POLICY STUDIES IN EMPLOYMENT AND WELFARE NUMBER 7

General Editors: Sar A. Levitan and Garth L. Mangum

Cooperatives and Rural Poverty in the South

Ray Marshall
Lamond Godwin

The Johns Hopkins Press, Baltimore and London

The Johns Hopkins Press, Baltimore, Maryland 21218
The Johns Hopkins Press Ltd., London

Library of Congress Catalog Card Number 70–135534

ISBN 0-8018-1232-1 (cloth)
ISBN 0-8018-1233-X (paper)

Originally published, 1971
Paperback edition, 1971

Contents

List of Tables

Preface

This book grew out of our research on the Negro in southern agriculture, as a part of the Negro Employment in the South Project, under a contract with the Manpower Administration of the U.S. Department of Labor, and our work as consultants for the Division of National Affairs of the Ford Foundation. Although it would be difficult to acknowledge the many debts we owe to people who have shaped our thinking and supported our work, we are especially grateful to Howard Rosen and Ellen Sehgal of the Office of Research, Manpower Administration, U.S. Department of Labor, and to Christopher Edley, George Esser, Hillary Feldstein, Eamon Kelley, Mitchell Sviridoff, Basil Whiting, and Roger Wilkins, all of the Ford Foundation. In the cooperatives, we benefited greatly from discussions with Father A. J. McKnight of the Southern Cooperative Development Program and Charles Prejean of the Federation of Southern Cooperatives. We are also grateful to John Gallman, Sar Levitan, and Garth Mangum for their valuable editorial suggestions.

Finally, we owe a great debt to our colleagues in the Negro Employment in the South Project, especially Virgil Christian, Carlos Erwin, and Adam Pepelasis, who are responsible for most of our statistics on employment in southern agriculture. A detailed study of the Negro in southern agriculture is forthcoming from the NES project, as well as studies of Negro employment in Atlanta, Birmingham, Louisville, Memphis, Miami, and New Orleans.[1] In addition to these city studies, special reports are forthcoming on Negro employment by the federal government and in state and local government. All of these studies have as their primary objectives analyses of Negro employment patterns and appraisals of various programs designed to improve black employment opportunities.

In spite of our heavy debts in the preparation of this monograph, we alone are responsible for any errors of fact or analysis, and the conclusions are entirely our own and do not necessarily represent the views of the Ford Foundation or the Manpower Administration of the U.S. Department of Labor.

[1] Vernon M. Briggs, Jr., "The Negro in the Houston Labor Market," The Negro Employment in the South Project series, No. 1. *Manpower Research Monograph*, No. 23, was published by the Manpower Administration, U.S. Department of Labor, in 1971.

Cooperatives and Rural Poverty in the South

1

Introduction

Because it is a complex problem with such long-range implications, it is not easy in a few words either to describe rural poverty in the South or to explain its causes. Per capita incomes are perhaps the best index of material welfare and will be examined later, but statistics alone cannot adequately depict the nature of the problem. Perhaps a better picture can be given by looking at the conditions of the children who suffer permanent damage because of poor educations, inadequate diets, and dilapidated housing. The health problems of the children of the rural poor are particularly serious, as indicated by the testimony of medical doctors who examined children in the region during the late 1960s.

For example, an investigation in Lowndes County, Alabama (which had 15,000 people and two doctors thirty-five miles apart), by a Yale Professor of Pediatrics in 1966 for the Tuskegee Institute Community Education Project found that

eighty percent of these children . . . had anemia sufficient to require treatment in any doctor's office anywhere in the country. [But] 90 percent of the children said they have never seen a doctor. One of those who answered "yes" to the question said: "Yes, he pulled my tooth."

1

. . . 25 percent of the children . . . needed further referral for glasses. One child out of 709 I examined had glasses.[1]

After a tour of the Mississippi Delta, a team of six medical doctors concluded:

We saw children who are hungry and who are sick—children for whom hunger is a daily fact of life and sickness, in many forms, an inevitability. We do not want to quibble over words, but "malnutrition" is not quite what we found; the boys and girls we saw were hungry—weak, in pain, sick; their lives are being shortened; they are, in fact, visibly and predictably losing their health, their energy, and their spirits. They are suffering from hunger and disease and directly or indirectly they are dying from them—which is exactly what "starvation" means.[2]

These conditions are all the more shocking in the light of increasing evidence that early malnutrition in children causes permanent damage to the development of intelligence.[3]

When they are older, many of the South's rural poor will escape to urban areas, as millions have done before them, but they will never completely recover from the physical and spiritual damage done them at an early age. Because they must attempt to compete for jobs in labor markets for which they are inadequately prepared or from which they are barred by racial discrimination, the South's rural poor become national problems. And the problem clearly has been aggravated by declining job opportunities in agriculture, as well as in other industries, for people with limited educations and skills.

Although the problems of the rural poor attracted considerable attention during the 1950s and 1960s, they are by no means new ones. The question therefore arises as to why they have persisted so long. Surely it cannot be because we knew so little about them, because they have been thoroughly documented by scores of scho-

[1] Paul Good, "Cycle to Nowhere," *Clearinghouse Publication No. 14* (Washington, D.C.: U.S. Commission on Civil Rights, 1968), p. 7.

[2] Joseph Bremmer et al., "Hungry Children," *Special Report* (Atlanta, Ga.: The Southern Regional Council, 1967), pp. 6–7.

[3] Nancy Hicks, "The Toll of Hunger on a Child's Intelligence," *New York Times,* March 1, 1970.

lars. However, scholarly studies alone cannot solve problems, nor can well-meaning policy makers whose understanding is limited to reading scholarly treaties. For example, New Deal agricultural policies failed to give adequate protection to tenants and sharecroppers when they had an excellent opportunity to carry out basic agricultural reforms, in spite of the well-meaning intentions of idealists who knew little—beyond what they had read—about the institutional arrangements of southern agriculture. (See David E. Conrad, *The Forgotten Farmers: Story of the Sharecroppers in the New Deal* [Urbana: University of Illinois Press, 1965].)

Poverty therefore persists in the rural South only partly because it is not visible to policy makers. The main reasons for the persistence of rural poverty relate to the poor people's powerlessness either to change their conditions directly or to influence public policy. We assume, in other words, that (1) the basic causes of rural poverty in the South are deeply entrenched and will require comprehensive remedies and (2) these comprehensive remedies are not likely to be either initiated or effective unless the rural poor and their political allies mount the kinds of pressures through organizations responsive to them to get better training and education, job opportunities, health and welfare programs, and housing. Moreover, effective measures must be taken to end racial discrimination in nonagricultural jobs in rural and urban areas and in the availability of credit and the purchase of land for blacks. Otherwise, the racial gaps will widen as poor blacks are unable to compete for rural or urban jobs.

This monograph is therefore based on the assumption that effective remedies to rural poverty are not likely unless the rural poor have organizations which can exert pressure for change. We see this as an important potential role of the cooperatives formed by the rural poor during the 1960s. However, we wish to emphasize at the outset that even if they become economically viable, we do not think cooperatives are either the only vehicles of pressure that can be formed or that they alone will be sufficient to make much of an impact on the causes of rural poverty. We believe the cooperatives are significant primarily because of their potential for

3

modest immediate improvements in the conditions of the rural poor (which nevertheless might be significant) and their potential for initiating really significant changes in public policies with respect to agriculture (including public policy on small farmers and the poor people's cooperatives themselves), economic development, education, manpower, welfare, and antidiscrimination programs.

However, a number of other organizations also might mobilize the kinds of pressure needed to stimulate effective public policies. These include political parties, nonprofit corporations, foundations, and labor organizations. Labor organizations might seem to have greater potential in southern agriculture now that Cesar Chavez and the National Farm Workers Union have successfully organized some agricultural workers in California. However, although agricultural unions might have some success in certain areas of the South, the prospects are not good for widespread adoption of collective bargaining by the region's agricultural workers and employers. Chavez succeeded in California in part because he was dealing with small, relatively homogeneous groups of workers in specialty crops which could be boycotted by consumers, but such tactics are less likely to succeed in the South's basic crops.

Thus, although we think unions and other organizations might be able to do something for those agricultural workers who can focus sufficient power on employers, the poor people's cooperatives formed during the 1960s probably have greater potential to become catalysts for rural institutional change than any other organizations currently on the scene.

This study seeks to clarify some of the basic issues concerning the role of these new enterprises as a means of improving the conditions of the rural poor and to examine their relationship to other economic development programs and approaches. First, the conditions responsible for poverty in the rural South are outlined. We then discuss the general nature of coops, the history of low-income coops in the South, and the emergence of the new poor people's cooperative movement. A representative sample of the new coops are then described in some detail. We conclude with an appraisal of the new coops.

We seek primarily to explore issues in this monograph rather than to evaluate the economic effectiveness of coops as antipoverty agencies. Proper evaluation, while highly desirable, must await more experience with these organizations and the accumulation of sufficient data to permit accurate appraisal.

RURAL POVERTY IN THE SOUTH[4]

The best overall indicator of the economic welfare of the South's people is their per capita income, which, largely because of problems of race and rural poverty, is below that of the rest of the United States, in spite of a long-range tendency for regional income gaps to narrow. In 1940, for example, per capita personal income in the South was 60 percent of the United States but was about 80 percent of the U.S. in 1969. Moreover, a much larger percentage of the South's people are poor than in the rest of the United States. In 1966, the Social Security Administration classified about 25 percent of the South's people as poor, as compared with 15 percent for the rest of the country.[5] Using the Social Security Administration's definition of poverty (based on family size and farm-nonfarm status rather than on a uniform national income level), Mollie Orshansky concluded that about half of the nation's poor were in the South in 1966.[6] Furthermore, poverty in the South is heavily concentrated in rural areas and among nonwhites. In 1966, the region accounted for a seventh of the nation's poor whites but two-thirds of its poor nonwhites. At that time, the average income of southern white families was five-sixths that of white families outside the South, while southern nonwhite incomes averaged only three-fifths that of nonwhites in other regions.

[4] In the remainder of this study, unless otherwise indicated, the South is defined as the states of the Confederacy plus Kentucky and Oklahoma.

[5] Mollie Orshansky, "Who Was Poor in 1966," *Research and Statistics Note*, U.S., Social Security Administration, Publication No. 23, Tables 5 and 6.

[6] "Counting the Poor: Another Look at the Poverty Profile," *Social Security Bulletin*, March 1968, pp. 5, 12.

One of the most disturbing trends in southern agriculture has been the tendency for the racial income gap to widen. Social Security data, which relate to the same individuals through time, indicate that even though Negro farmers earned less than half as much as whites in 1960, they gained only $76 in income ($1,371 to $1,447) between 1960 and 1965 as compared with $1,025 for non-Negroes ($2,734 to $3,759).[7] Since Negro farm operators' incomes went up on the average only about as much as the increase in the cost of living, we can conclude that these individuals made no gains in their real incomes during these years.

The origins of rural poverty in the South and the special problems of rural black people are deeply rooted in the region's past. Indeed, as Rostow pointed out, the South is the only region of the nation which had what could be called a "traditional" society in terms of economic development.[8]

Institutionalized racism together with the sharecropping system gave little opportunity or incentive for black farmers to improve either themselves or the land they farmed. The sharecroppers were usually in debt for their supplies to a merchant or a planter and paid very high prices for their supplies and high interests on their debts. Since most sharecroppers were illiterate, they were unable to detect chicanery which cheated them of their earnings. Cotton, corn, and tobacco were the most marketable crops, so debt-ridden sharecroppers were restricted to the production of these staples and got little experience producing other crops. Shamefully inferior schools and discrimination in nonagricultural employment made it very difficult for blacks to escape the cycle of rural poverty, except during periods when extreme labor shortages made it necessary for white employers to hire blacks after the available supply of foreign and domestic whites was exhausted.

---

[7] Calculated from a 1 percent sample of persons covered by the Old Age, Survivors, and Disability Insurance Act.

[8] W. W. Rostow, *Stages of Economic Development* (Cambridge: At the University Press, 1960), p. 18.

Migration

Thus, the cessation of European immigration and labor shortages caused by the entrance of young whites into the military during World War I made it possible for increasing numbers of blacks to leave the rural South. The attraction of urban jobs in the North and the hardships they faced in the South (hardships made even worse during the 1920s by soil erosion and the ravages of the boll weevil) caused a steady decline in the numbers of black farmers thereafter (table 1).

Table 1.   Negro Farm Operators in the United States, 1900–1964

Area	1920	1940	1950	1959	1964
United States	925,708	681,790	559,980	272,541	184,004
Northeast	1,469	1,432	1,002	596	334
North Central	7,911	7,466	6,700	4,259	1,796
South	915,595	672,214	551,469	267,008	180,418
West	735	678	809	678	554
Southern states	907,991	666,866	547,184	264,562	170,889

Source: U.S. Bureau of the Census, *Census of Agriculture, 1959*, Vol. II; *Census of Agriculture, 1964*, Vol. II.

The migration of blacks out of the rural South also was accelerated by U.S. agricultural policies during the 1930s and mechanization during the early forties. Indeed, the most significant declines in black population of the rural South came after World War II.[9] The total number of farms of all types operated by blacks in the nation was 184,004 in 1964, a significant decrease from the peak of 925,170 in 1920. Fifty-six percent of the black farms in the South in 1964 were operated on some form of share-tenant basis as compared with only 19 percent for whites.

Black farmers, traditionally, have specialized in such labor-intensive cash crops as cotton and tobacco. According to Census of Agriculture figures, more than half (56 percent) of all black commercial farmers in 1959 were cotton producers, and 26 percent

[9] U.S., Bureau of Economic Research Report No. 101 (1966), *Rural People in the American Economy*, p. 51.

of them were tobacco growers. In 1964, about half (58,793) of the 116,785 nonwhite farmers in the South were still producing cotton, and more than a fourth of them continued to grow tobacco. These crops have been adversely affected by governmental policies and technological changes which have restricted production and reduced the demand for labor. For example, whereas 92 percent of all cotton in the United States was harvested by hand in 1950, only 11 percent was handpicked in 1966 because of the introduction of the mechanical harvester and new methods of weed control. Only 20 percent of the cotton produced in the South was harvested by hand in 1966 as compared with 52 percent in 1962.

Tobacco has not been mechanized to the same extent as cotton, but the number of black tobacco farmers dropped from 91,000 in 1945 to 31,000 in 1964. Moreover, technological changes in harvesting and curing tobacco which have already been tested will greatly reduce labor requirements in the future and will make it more difficult for small farmers to compete.

Black farmers were more vulnerable to displacement than white farmers primarily because their inadequate incomes, education, experience, and capital made it difficult for them to take advantage of technological changes. Moreover, they did not have enough political and economic power to overcome racial discrimination in the administration of government agricultural programs. Indeed, it was the rich and powerful white farmers who benefited from these programs, usually at the expense of their poor tenants.[10]

It is very important to note that the decline in the Negro farm population has *not* been accompanied by a corresponding decline in the rural nonfarm population. The rural black population had *declined* in each decade since 1920 while the black rural nonfarm population was *increasing* in every decade. In 1920, for example, 6.9 million Negroes lived in rural areas, 5.1 million of whom were on the farms and 1.8 million of whom were nonfarm. By 1960, only 2.4 million Negroes lived on farms while 2.7 million were

[10] Arthur M. Schlesinger, Jr., *The Coming of the New Deal* (Boston: Houghton Mifflin Co., 1959), p. 77; Gunnar Myrdal, *An American Dilemma* (New York: Harper & Bros., 1944), p. 256.

rural nonfarm; 93 percent of the nation's rural black population was in the South.[11] Any economic development policy in the rural South must therefore give considerable attention to the rural non-farm population.

THE FUTURE OF THE NEGRO IN SOUTHERN AGRICULTURE

The future of poor people's cooperatives in the rural South obviously will depend heavily on what happens to small black farmers, which is problematical. Much depends on technological developments and the Negroes' success in obtaining income-earning opportunities in agriculture and nonagricultural occupations. Much also depends on public policies in agriculture as well as in economic and human resource development.

The technological revolution in cotton production is nearly complete, as indicated by aggregate man-hours in production in 1966 that are only 14 percent as great as in 1940,[12] but, as noted earlier, future labor use in tobacco is uncertain. In 1968 total labor requirements in southern agriculture were only about 40 percent, in man-hours, of the 1951 level. If this trend continued, the 1975 man-hour labor requirements will be only about 35 percent of the 1951 level.[13]

Another problem for agricultural workers has been growing underemployment, especially of blacks. In 1950, 2.74 million white workers filled 1.96 million jobs, or, there were about seven jobs for every ten workers. By 1969, 1.19 million white farm workers filled 59 million jobs, meaning less than five jobs for ten workers. There were about 767,000 nonwhite family farm workers in 1950

[11] *Rural People in the American Economy*, p. 53.

[12] U.S., Department of Agriculture Statistical Bulletin No. 233 (June 1967), *Changes in Farm Production and Efficiency, A Summary Report*, p. 13. Man-hours are reduced to a homogeneous equivalent in the series and reflect the labor needed to produce the actual output.

[13] *Ibid.* The 1975 projection was generated by straightforward extrapolation of an exponential decay curve of the $Yc = k + ab^x$ fitted to this series. In numerical terms, the equation is $Yc = 2135 + (5108) \ x \ (.8917)^x$, x measured in number of years from mid-year, 1951.

9

and 540,000 nonwhite full-time jobs, about the same ratio of workers to jobs as for whites. However, by 1969, there were about 158,000 nonwhite workers and only 73,000 full-time jobs, a ratio of about 4.6 jobs for every ten workers.[14]

Black farmers also have been displaced at a much greater rate than white farmers.[15] In 1950 there were three black for every ten whites, but by 1969 there was less than one black for every seven whites. Thus there were approximately 30 percent as many white farmers in 1969 as in 1950 but only 13 percent as many blacks.

The number of hired farm workers also dropped sharply from 1,043,000 in 1950 to 513,000 in 1969. The decline of 530,000 amounts to roughly 453,000 full-time jobs. The 438,000 full-time jobs in 1969 were split almost equally between the races, with whites having a slight edge: 52.7 percent in 1966; 50.9 percent in 1967; 55.1 percent in 1968.[16]

Migration

Population trends suggest great movements of people in and out of the South during the 1950s and 1960s: out-migration of displaced agricultural workers unable to find nonagricultural jobs; immigration of skilled labor needed in the South's growth industries; net out-migration, on balance, because employment in the nonagricultural sectors did not expand sufficiently in the job categories required to take care of the shift from agriculture added to the natural increase in the labor force. Migration data bear out these propositions, but they also indicate a much more complex story.

---

[14] Calculated from USDA Statistical Bulletins No. 316 (June 1962) and No. 334 (1963); USDA Crop Reporting Board, *Farm Labor*, 1963 to present; data for reduction of full-time equivalents came from the 1954, 1959, and 1964 Census of Agriculture. Intercensal years were computed by linear interpolation between census years.

[15] Operators and unpaid family workers.

[16] Department of Agriculture, Agricultural Economic Report a 93.28, Nos. 120, 148, and 164. These percentages are for the Census South, which probably overstates the white proportion of jobs in the South as defined in this study.

In particular, the data reveal strong intraregional variation and lend support to the notion that the lure of a better life out of the South was very strong for Negroes of all educational levels in the early fifties.

A factor of considerable significance for the future of the poor people's coops, however, is the conclusion that the South's rural population *may not continue* to decline during the 1970s as fast as it did in previous decades. For one thing, the small black farm population (1,408,000 in 1965) means that farm population losses may no longer offset increases in the rural nonfarm population. Indeed, there is considerable evidence that net out-migration of blacks from the South declined significantly during the late 1960s. Moreover, future population growth is influenced by the fact that rural blacks have much larger families than urban blacks or whites or rural whites. Although public policies, such as the Family Assistance Plan, might change these population trends, the rural black population of the South is likely to remain almost unchanged and might even increase during the 1970s.

Nonagricultural Employment

Employment in the nonagricultural sectors of the South, which has expanded markedly since 1950, will influence the Negro's future in southern agriculture by providing or denying alternative employment opportunities. Unfortunately, however, the movement of poor people out of the rural South is impeded by the poor matchup between the qualifications of displaced farm labor and the requirements of the South's growth industries. Indeed, 92.8 percent of black farm males in 1960 had less than a high school education, 82.2 percent had less than eight years, and 53.5 percent had less than five years. For white farm males, the picture was somewhat better but far from encouraging: 71.4 percent had less than high school, 46.4 percent less than eight years, and 19.0 percent less than five years.[17] Adjusting for differences in the equality of

[17] Mary Jean Bowman, "Human Inequalities and Southern Underdevelopment," *The Southern Economic Journal Supplement of Education and the Southern Economy,* July 1965, p. 75.

education, we conclude that over 80 percent of the black males who left southern agriculture between 1950 and 1969 had less than an effective seventh grade education, and well over half had less than four years of school.[18]

The supply side of the nonagricultural labor market was therefore swelled by almost 600,000 black males who were not prepared to go into the South's expanding nonagricultural jobs. Census data show years of schooling in 1960 for males in the most rapidly growing southern industries to have ranged from 8.04 years in mining to 17.21 for professionals.[19] Even the rapidly growing apparel industry had a median of 10.3 years.[20]

When combined with our analysis of the Negro's position in agriculture, these data on nonagricultural employment do not cause great optimism about the economic future of Negroes displaced from southern agriculture, unless public policies change these trends. Clearly, therefore, if the unemployment and underemployment of black males is to be reduced, policies must be adopted to make it possible for Negroes to use their training and experience for agricultural jobs, to upgrade their skills, or to be employed in public jobs.

Agricultural Policies

However, there also is very little evidence that the Negro's future in agriculture is being significantly improved by federal poli-

[18] James S. Coleman, *Equality of Educational Opportunity*, U.S., Department of Health, Education and Welfare (Washington: U.S. Government Printing Office, 1966), p. 273.

[19] Of course, it would be useful to know entry-level requirements to industries, but this information is not available.

[20] Data from the 1960 census of population. The median years of schooling were taken for the typical SIC in each case. The complete picture is as follows: professional and related services (SICs 80 and 81), 17.21 and 17.31 years, respectively; wholesale and retail trade (50 and 53), 11.84 and 12.03; construction (15, 16, and 17), 8.80, 8.80, and 8.80; government (91, 92, and 93), 12.46, 12.53, and 11.15; finance, insurance, and real estate (60, 62, and 65), 12.90, 14.55, and 12.06; business and repair services (73 and 76), 12.29 and 10.34; apparel products manufacturing (23), 10.30; food and kindred products (20), 9.48.

cies. Indeed, in many ways, the conditions of small farmers in the South have been worsened by agricultural programs. Although justified on the grounds of "parity," these programs continue to help those most who need the least help. The more affluent interests have been able to perpetuate their control over agricultural policy through a constellation of political and economic powers extending from Congress to the local sheriff's office. Because of the predominantly one-party political system in the South and congressional seniority, rural white southerners have controlled key agricultural committees in Congress and have seen to it that the U.S. Department of Agriculture reflected their racist desires and economic interests.

Although there were the beginnings of some improvements during the late 1960s, the pervasiveness and persistence of racial discrimination in programs administered by the U.S. Department of Agriculture have been thoroughly documented by the U.S. Commission on Civil Rights (USCOCR).[21]

Conclusions

As noted at the outset of this discussion, it is impossible to predict the future of small black and white farmers in southern agriculture. Much depends on whether present trends continue, which in turn will depend heavily upon U.S. agriculture policies and the success or failure of various human resource development programs currently under way.

If the small white farmer's future is bleak, the small Negro farmer's plight clearly is even worse. American experts believe that there is little chance for the Negro to survive in American agriculture. For example, Schultz argues: "American Negroes have long been suppressed in agriculture" by white people and the USDA. "In sharp contrast, our central cities have been preparing the stage despite all manner of stresses and strains so that Negroes

[21] U.S., Commission on Civil Rights, *Equal Opportunity in Farm Programs* (Washington: U.S. Government Printing Office, 1965), pp. 100–101.

can become first class citizens. Future historians will no doubt discover that Negroes, like Jews, have found in cities protection and opportunity denied to them in the countryside."[22] Schultz also is convinced that, given a choice, most Negroes would prefer to get out of agriculture, which to them is an inferior occupation. "These cultural values are deeply rooted in the history of slavery and the failure of agricultural institutions since emancipation to grant them social status, human dignity, civil rights, schooling, and economic opportunity."[23]

Beale agrees with Schultz's appraisal of the Negroes' prospects and attitudes but holds out at least a little hope for their survival.

> Observers in the South, both white and Negro, express the opinion that the prospect of farming in the rural South has become emotionally unattractive to most rural Negro youth. It is urban and especially metropolitan life that has status. . . .
>
> To be optimistic about the future of Negro farmers would be to disregard almost every facet of their past and present status. But then, the odds have always been against them even in the period when they reached their greatest numbers.[24]

However, Beale thinks a larger number of black farmers might survive if their land could be combined into larger units, if federal programs were adopted to permit small Negro farmers to purchase land, or if additional nonfarm employment became available to rural Negroes.

---

[22] Theodore W. Schultz, "National Employment, Skills, and Earnings of Farm Labor" in C. E. Bishop (ed.), *Farm Labor in the United States* (New York: Columbia University Press, 1967), p. 61.

[23] *Ibid.*, p. 61–62.

[24] Calvin L. Beale, "The Negro in American Agriculture" in John P. Davis (ed.), *The American Negro Reference Book* (Englewood Cliffs, N.J.: Prentice-Hall, Inc., 1966), p. 200.

2

Cooperatives and Rural Development

As noted in the previous chapter, the future of small farmers in the United States is not very bright, and that of black farmers is bleaker still, unless present trends are changed. Moreover, these trends are not likely to change, even under the most favorable circumstances, unless poor people initiate changes through organizations that they control. In the rural South, the main economic organizations representing poor people are the cooperatives, which have had varying degrees of success elsewhere. By first looking at the nature of cooperatives and their use in other places as vehicles for rural development, we will be in a much better position to appraise cooperatives in the rural South, which we do in chapters 3 and 4.

THE NATURE OF COOPERATIVES

A cooperative is a type of business firm which has three distinguishing characteristics:

1) A coop is owned and controlled by its member-customers on a democratic basis. Each member usually has one vote, but in some cases votes are allocated to members on the basis of patron-

age. This distinguishes coops from corporations, which allocate control and voting rights in proportion to the capital invested by stockholders, who may or may not be customers of the firm.

2) Cooperatives differ from other businesses in the manner in which surplus earnings are distributed. The net margin over costs is returned to customers in proportion to their patronage and not in proportion to their capital investment. These returns are called patronage refunds. This technique usually enables members and patrons to obtain goods and/or services at lower prices and returns on investments at higher prices than those received or paid by customers of other types of firms.

3) Membership in a coop is voluntary. Coops are organized to serve the needs of their members, whereas other commerical firms are organized to earn profits and returns on invested capital. The coop's primary purpose is to help its members realize higher incomes, lower costs, or more efficient and dependable service.

Coops and Rural Development

As voluntary associations formed by people to satisfy their needs more effectively than they could as individuals, cooperatives have been important instruments for rural development throughout the world, and the rate of growth of rural cooperatives has been rapid during the past twenty years, particularly in the poorer nations.

The kind of cooperatives which have been most useful for agricultural development include:

1) *Land associations*, which may buy land for sale or lease to members, provide a source of credit for members to buy land, or establish collective farms. In general, landholding societies have not been too successful because of individual differences (family sizes, skill, motivation, etc.), and problems in adjusting to change (such as terms under which members withdraw and changing family composition). Where they exist, as in China, Israel, or the Soviet Union, collective farms are held together more by political, religious, or ideological than economic considerations. However, co-

operatives can and have been important adjuncts to land reform and individual farming systems.

2) *Associations for educational or technical training* have ordinarily been federations or unions of other cooperatives and have geared education, training, and cultural programs to the needs and interests of their members.

3) *Credit and savings* coops are extremely important. A United Nations survey concluded that "of all the services which voluntary cooperative associations have undertaken for farmer members, that of obtaining and administering credit is, in most countries, the one they have carried out best."[1] As credit agencies, cooperatives have had the advantage of fairly intimate knowledge of their members' character and circumstances as well as of local production possibilities. Since they often rely heavily on volunteers and have simple procedures, they minimize administrative costs. Moreover, as voluntary associations, cooperatives have been able to instill confidence in small rural farmers, especially when cooperative credit institutions use a *supervised credit* approach. Under supervised credit, staff experts from the lending institutions work very closely with borrowers in formulating their credit needs and helping them to acquire the technical assistance and capital inputs needed to successfully carry out the activities for which the credit is obtained. This approach is particularly important in dealing with poor farmers with limited educations and managerial abilities. It is a form of participatory education which is expensive of staff time, but without which many projects would become much more risky. Supervised credit also is based upon the assumption that credit is only one part of a total package of things needed by farmers for economic success.

Supervised credit by cooperative lending agencies can also rely on criteria for making loans which are different from those used by commercial financial institutions. The latter will attempt to maximize profits, which ordinarily means that they will ration their financial resources to people on the basis of the greatest potential gains and

---

[1] United Nations, *Rural Progress through Cooperatives,* 1954, p. 37.

lowest risks. This is a good way to make private profits, but it will not necessarily promote economic or human resource development. The cooperative credit institution, on the other hand, is not a profit making institution and is primarily interested in meeting its members' credit needs. It can therefore use prospective earnings and the character of the borrower, rather than assets, as bases for making loans. Of course, the cooperative must also be interested in the safety of its loans, but it need not be concerned with the greatest returns for those loans. It is commonly assumed that if loans in rural areas were profitable, private investors would take advantage of them. But loans can be profitable in the sense that borrowers can use them to produce more than the cost of the loan and still not be profitable enough to attract private investors. Moreover, the argument that private investors will respond to profitable investments in rural areas assumes a perfect capital market, which is not the case. Rural credit institutions might have monopolies, because of government charters, which enables them to ration credit to large borrowers and to ignore smaller ones or to discriminate against borrowers for racial, political, or ideological reasons. As in other activities, cooperatives can counteract these private monopolies and reduce the costs of credit.

Cooperative credit institutions also have some disadvantages as compared with private financial institutions. They are particularly likely to be handicapped by shortages of credit and a lack of experienced management, and their operations are likely to be inflexible and time consuming because they rely on committees and volunteers. Poor farmers, in particular, might have limited understanding of the nature and uses of credit.

4) *Supply societies* also can benefit poor farmers, who often pay high prices for the goods and services they consume or use on their farms. These high prices are caused by many factors, including the risks involved in selling to poor farmers, the high costs of getting goods and services to them, the need to add credit costs to the prices of goods and services, and the fact that local traders might enjoy monopolies in their trading areas because many suppliers of goods and services are not interested in competing in rural

markets. Cooperatives can therefore form various kinds of associations (livestock breeding, machinery, small-scale industries, consumer store or buying clubs, insurance and health societies, and cooperative housing associations) to centralize the demands of the members, realize economies of scale, provide consumer education, break local monopolies, and provide technical knowledge for their members.

However, cooperatives might not always be able to do these things better than private businesses. They have some advantages as compared with private traders in that they need not make profits and can assure a market and minimize costs, but they also have disadvantages. Private firms might be able to attract better management and might have more flexibility in their operations because they do not have to go through the democratic process. Moreover, cooperative supply organizations have had difficulty surviving where there was no clear need for the service; a lack of homogeneous membership needs and interests; inadequate capital; inexperienced or untrained staffs; and poor record keeping, inventory control, and credit policies. These difficulties often can be overcome with the help of central cooperative federations or wholesale societies, but they have plagued rural coops throughout their history.

5) *Marketing and processing associations* have provided some of the most valuable services to farmers by helping them receive greater net returns on their products. There are many reasons why farmers have received low prices: inability to control the quantity and quality of the supplies sold; imperfect knowledge of markets; poor transportation and storage facilities, which prevent them from taking advantage of the best prices; and imperfect competition among buyers of farm products. Cooperatives sometimes have overcome these disadvantages, but they may not have advantages over private traders because the latter might have greater access to capital and management ability. However, cooperatives have sometimes been successful in negotiating higher prices for farm products simply by threatening to market themselves.

6) Cooperatives also have been formed for such purposes as building self-help housing, securing rural health services, providing insurance against risks, and promoting education and training. Many of these miscellaneous services are sometimes provided by associations, like federations, unions. or wholesale societies, formed by individual cooperatives.

CONDITIONS FOR SUCCESS

Experience around the world indicates that a number of factors must ordinarily be present in order for all kinds of cooperatives to be economic successes:

1) A basic requirement for economic success among cooperatives is social cohesion, which may be produced by religious, racial, patriotic, or ideological considerations. In some cases, coops have catered to particular ethnic groups because the inclusion of different groups prevents unity. In Israel, for example, the Moshav, or agricultural settlement based on family farms and cooperatives, at first tried integrating different ethnic groups, but this caused trouble and led to the adoption of a different social theory, recognizing "that assimilation is a slow process and that speed in assimilation may be sacrificed to community stability."[2] Social cohesion is important because it facilitates the mutual confidence necessary for democratic control.

2) The services provided by the cooperative must be in strong and continuous demand by the members. If the cooperative is not based on strongly felt membership needs or if members can obtain greater benefits from private traders, the society will have difficulty surviving.

3) Good management is one of the most important ingredients of successful cooperatives and one of the most common causes of failure among poor farmers' associations.

4) The coop must be able to meet political and economic opposition from those who feel threatened by its objectives.

[2] Maxwell I. Klayman, *The Moshav in Israel* (New York: Praeger, 1970).

5) The coop ordinarily requires a favorable economic environment and must have the ability to survive economic adversity.

6) The amount and character of outside help often is crucial to the success of cooperatives, particularly in early stages. Help might come from governments, federations of cooperatives, foundations, or sympathetic organizations and individuals.

COOPERATIVES AND NONECONOMIC OBJECTIVES

Although cooperatives have a wide range of economic uses, they also have formed the basis for movements to improve the social position of groups of people and even nations, a role for which they are ideally suited because of their democratic structure and patron-oriented motivation. However, although a coop often has social and political objectives, these objectives cannot be achieved unless the coop is an economic success.

Established American farm coops have been primarily economic organizations which have relied for the most part on "supply management" in order to control markets and protect farm incomes. They consequently take a very dim view of combining economic and social objectives because the latter might weaken the coop economically. For example, poor farmers are not welcomed as members because of their economic weakness.

COOPERATIVES AND FARM SIZE

The economic future of small farmers clearly has important implications for the development of cooperatives. Their advocates argue that coops can make it possible for small farmers to acquire the advantages of large-scale production and marketing techniques while maintaining family farms. However, there is an opinion among American authorities that small family farms are obsolete and that cooperatives have little to offer poor farmers. The proponents of large-scale farming, whether corporate or collective, argue that modern technology makes large enterprises much more

21

efficient, profitable, and practical than small family farms. According to Higbee, for example,

a social institution cannot live out of context and the old context has been demolished by the growth of mass populations. Smallness is out; bigness is in. New systems of mass production are needed to satisfy the mass needs of a vastly multiplied and urbanized humanity. . . .

The small farmer can no longer establish contact with the small consumer on a scale required to feed the population. Food must be assembled by the trainload rather than by the wagonload, and transported across the continent rather than across a township. This calls for a new gigantism in production and distribution. A few small farmers may survive by lying between the rails as the freights thunder by, but they are becoming as rare as old-fashioned butchershops in an age of supermarkets.[3]

Although Higbee considers supply management coops to be "organized agriculture's best effective economic weapon,"[4] he makes it clear that poor farmers cannot play the "supply management" game: "The discipline necessary to produce a standardized output must begin on the farm, and thus it is that the coops often act as filter, admitting to membership or to favorable quota status only those farmers who can comply with rigid specifications. . . . The poor and unsophisticated cannot play this game; they are too numerous, they lack credit, and they lack perception."[5]

Higbee concludes that poor farmers "need help and they need it badly, but they cannot expect to become genuine farmers because they would require capital which they do not have and cannot get. Their future is not in agriculture but in occupations where someone else can supply the capital necessary to create the decent jobs."[6]

Other American observers agree with Higbee. For example, Fred Bailey, Jr., concludes that "the small farm [is] moving steadily and rapidly toward numerical extinction. . . . Nor have so-called 'rural

[3] Edward Higbee, *Farms and Farmers in an Urban Age* (New York: The Twentieth Century Fund, 1963), p. 4.
[4] *Ibid.*, p. 35.
[5] *Ibid.*, pp. 36–37.
[6] *Ibid.*, p. 48.

development' programs . . . achieved any widespread success in providing the small farmer a practical alternative to farming."[7]

However, other observers believe that small family farms can survive, especially where they are supported by viable cooperative movements and combine with other income-earning opportunities in rural areas. Moreover, in this view, large farms in the United States have been stimulated by American agricultural policies which greatly favor large farmers at the expense of small ones. Co-operative advocates concede that small family-owned farms have disadvantages in marketing and production but argue that some of these can be overcome through cooperatives. Defenders of family farms also contend that owner-occupied units have advantages which come from pride of ownership, willingness to invest and to improve one's own land, close and intimate supervision, and flexibility.[8]

Another aspect of the large versus small farm controversy concerns efficiency in the use of labor. The economics of labor use is quite different on family and large commercial farms. On the latter, the labor market determines labor utilizations. Labor is therefore utilized in such a way as to maximize profits; this means equating wages with the contribution to revenue of the marginal amount of employment. Those who cannot be hired at this wage must either accept lower wages or be unemployed. In a perfectly competitive market, unemployment would drive wages down, and there would be full employment. However, the labor market is not perfect. Where minimum wages are fixed by law, as in the United States, the legal minimum limits the extent to which workers can lower their wages.

On small family farms, the market plays a much different role in labor utilization. Prevailing wages become relevant as opportunity costs only if workers can find jobs at prevailing wages. Because of a declining demand for the kinds of workers who are being displaced in southern agriculture, there might be no jobs available to those

[7] See Fred Bailey, Jr., "The Nation's Two Agricultures," *Banking,* March 1968, p. 84.

[8] See, for example, Klayman, *The Moshav in Israel,* p. 266.

workers at prevailing wages. It can be argued, of course, that programs should be adopted to qualify these workers for jobs that are available, but these programs are not suitable for many displaced southern agrarians. As a consequence, the opportunity cost of labor to these farm families becomes very low, making it possible for them to compete in labor intensive activities with larger farmers for whom the legal minimum, or market, wage is relevant. This conclusion also means that low-wage jobs and income maintenance programs which provide incomes that are marginal by urban standards are likely to appear fairly attractive to displaced agrarians who have few job alternatives.

From a social point of view, the benefits of small farms or other marginal income-earning activities might be greater than the public costs of subsidizing their preservation. The large market-oriented agribusinesses will not always pay wages sufficient to support its workers, because the demand for labor in agriculture has always been seasonal. Entrepreneurs might be willing to pay wages which are relatively high for the time actually worked, but workers must live year round. In this system, the worker is required to bear the full cost of seasonality or to shift part of it to governments in the form of welfare. If these workers were able to engage in family farming and/or other subsidized productive activity which would pay them an amount at least equal to the poverty level, it might make economic sense for the government to subsidize them if the alternative public costs were lower than the amount of the subsidies to small farmers or small rural industries.

Much of the literature relating to the alleged economic advantages of large-scale farming assumes that there are significant economies of scale. Although some American research supports economies of scale for some crops, the evidence does not reveal across-the-board advantages to large farms.[9]

[9] Don Kanel, *Size of Farm and Economic Development*, Land Tenure Center Reprint No. 31 (Madison: University of Wisconsin, 1967); K. L. Bachman and E. P. Christensen, "The Economics of Farm Size," in Herman Southworth and Bruce F. Johnston (eds.), *Agricultural Development and Economic Growth* (Ithaca: Cornell University Press, 1967); cited by Klayman, *The Moshav in Israel,* p. 370.

Even if a case could be made on microeconomic grounds for the survival and subsidization of small farms, national decisions must also consider the macroeconomic aspects as well. One argument against subsidizing small farms is that this will cause greater damage to all farmers than the gain to the small farmers.[10] This argument assumes an inelastic overall demand for agricultural products (and a low and declining income elasticity of demand), which means that increasing aggregate supply will reduce total farm revenue. Whether this should be a significant public policy consideration depends upon the effect of the overall reduction in the incomes of large farmers on national policy. It could be argued that the subsidy is good for consumers because it increases food supplies and lowers their costs. Most U.S. agriculture policies subsidize capital and not labor. However, if large farmers are more efficient in the production of certain crops, it is difficult for us to see why they should be subsidized. On the other hand, subsidies to small farmers and cooperatives formed by them might be necessary to help them switch out of capital intensive crops, where many of them have been concentrated as tenants or agricultural workers before they become mechanized, into those requiring less capital. Coops can be used both for those kinds of capital requirements which complement labor—fertilizer, improved seed varieties, etc.—as well as those which are labor saving. If the latter are indivisible, such as large harvesting or grading equipment or breeding stock, they can be owned cooperatively by groups of small farmers.

In order to be used as an instrument to help the rural poor, it could well be that the cooperative will have to be modified, at least as it has traditionally operated in the United States. Fortunately, however, these associations have proved to be fairly flexible institutions to meet the needs of people under a wide variety of circumstances, even though some experts feel that the basic principles must be rigidly adhered to or the organization cannot properly be called a cooperative.[11]

[10] Bailey, "The Nation's Two Agricultures," p. 86.
[11] See Ewell Paul Ray, *Cooperatives Today and Tomorrow* (Danville, Ill.: Interstate Publishers and Promoters, 1964), p. 111.

The foregoing is not meant to imply that the experience in other countries is necessarily applicable to the problems of the rural South, but it is intended to show that any organizational structure must be shaped by the realities of local institutions and situations. Moreover, we are persuaded that useful insights into solutions for American problems can be gained by making international comparisons, especially when unique circumstances in each country are accounted for. We conclude from the international experience on farm size that large farms have advantages for some kinds of farming, but we are not persuaded by that evidence that large farms are technically or economically superior for all activities. We conclude, moreover, that small farmers can gain some of the advantages of both small-scale operations (to which they are committed by necessity) and large-scale marketing and purchasing activities if they can form cooperatives.

COOPERATIVES IN THE UNITED STATES

Although cooperatives have had a long history in American agriculture dating back to the early 1800s,[12] they did not begin in the South until the end of the nineteenth century. However, by 1915, cooperatives had been established in nearly every state in the nation.[13] Beginning about 1920, large-scale cooperative marketing of farm commodities reached a high level of development, and a number of statewide, regional, and national organizations were formed (including the American Farm Bureau Federation, the American Institute for Cooperation, the National Council of Farmers Cooperatives, the National Federation of Grain Cooperatives, and the Cooperative League).

During the New Deal years, numerous federal and state laws facilitating cooperatives were enacted. The federal government made it possible for farmers to secure short-term credit cooperatively, and a special banking system for coops was established. A

[12] *Ibid.*, p. 56.
[13] *Ibid.*, p. 59.

federal credit union act was passed which permitted the federal chartering of credit unions.[14] By 1952 there were 10,166 farmers' cooperatives of all kinds, with a total membership of 7,636,000 (as compared with three million members in 1932) and a gross business volume of 12.1 billion dollars.[15] In 1966, when the latest count was made, nearly 8,400 agricultural cooperatives with 6.9 million members grossed almost 21 billion dollars, net business volume was 15.6 billion dollars, and five regional farm coops were among the 500 largest U.S. corporations in sales.[16]

American cooperatives have traditionally been most successful among particular groups, especially the large- and middle-sized farmers who have had the land, capital, and entrepreneurial skills necessary to establish successful businesses.

Consumer cooperatives have been strong in the United States mainly in areas where Scandinavians have settled. Credit unions, savings and loan associations, and mutual insurance companies, all financial institutions based on cooperative principles, are more pervasive throughout the nation. As contrasted with Europe, consumer cooperatives in the United States have been relatively weak for a variety of reasons, including: the strength and efficiency of chain stores in the United States, which, because of a vast internal market, could exercise countervailing power against producers and give consumers relatively low prices (however, this power has caused farmers' marketing coops to be formed in self-defense); the strength of private traders and their opposition to cooperatives; and the absence of strong class or ideological movements supporting cooperatives.[17] Furthermore, higher average incomes in the

[14] R. H. Ellsworth, *The Story of Farmers' Cooperatives* (Washington: Farm Credit Administration, 1938), pp. 4–7.

[15] Anne L. Gessner, "Statistics of Farmers, Marketing, Purchasing, and Service Cooperatives, 1951–1952," *Farmers Cooperative Service Report No. 2* (Washington, D.C., 1954), p. 14.

[16] *Cooperatives in the United States: Facts and Figures* (Chicago: The Cooperative League of the United States, 1967), p. 15.

[17] See Jack Bailey, *The Cooperative Movement* (London: Labour Party), Educational Series, No. 2, August 1952.

27

United States have caused many consumers to be less concerned than Europeans with maximizing their purchasing power.

In general, the American cooperative movement has had very little to offer the poor farmer with inadequate incomes and assets. The following chapter outlines the development of cooperatives among small black farmers in the United States.

3

The Poor People's Cooperative Movement

Cooperatives have a number of advantages in helping people to help themselves and therefore could do much to meet the educational, political, and economic needs of poor people in the rural South. The cooperative's organizational structure provides for equal and democratic control of management and risk taking, which is an ideal means of involving poor people in planning for their own needs. Membership meetings, when properly conducted, demonstrate the advantages of free and open discussion and provide for personal development as well as for technical and economic education. In addition, as experiences in other countries illustrate, coops can be used to develop political leadership.[1] Moreover by providing greater economic independence, coops could make their members less vulnerable to the use of economic pressures against them for political purposes.

HISTORY OF POOR PEOPLE'S COOPS IN THE RURAL SOUTH

There have been a number of attempts to establish successful cooperatives among low-income farmers in the South, dating back

[1] See, for example, F. Ray Marshall, "The Finnish Cooperative Movement," *Land Economics*, August 1958; and Maxwell I. Klayman, *The Moshav in Israel* (New York: Praeger, 1970).

29

to the nineteenth century. Some of the earliest efforts were in the 1880s and 1890s by the Farmers Alliance (FA), a radical agrarian protest organization formed in Texas in 1872. This group established several low-income cooperatives in the South, the most important of which was the Farmers Alliance Exchange, organized in Dallas to market cotton.[2] The FA restricted its membership to whites but was affiliated with the Colored Farmers Alliance and Cooperative Union (CFACU), also formed in Texas by a white Baptist preacher in 1886.[3] Like the white Farmers Alliance, the CFACU promoted the development of poor people's coops and, at its peak, claimed to have had more than one million members spread throughout the South.[4] Although the economic programs of the FA and the CFACU were similar, there were crucial differences in the political platforms of these two groups. For example, the CFACU strongly supported legislative proposals (such as the Lodge Federal Election Bill) which were designed to guarantee the voting rights of black southerners in national elections through the use of federal troops. The white FA was not only strongly opposed to this proposal but also supported discriminatory legislation.[5] The most serious disagreement between the two groups resulted from a strike by black cotton pickers called by the CFACU in 1891. This strike was strongly opposed by the white Farmers Alliance, many of whose members were employers of the striking black cotton pickers. The strike finally ended in defeat for the black pickers, and the CFACU was out of existence by the end of 1891.[6]

During roughly the same period, the Knights of Labor and the Populists attempted to organize racially integrated unions and poor people's cooperatives. Indeed, some Populist leaders were so bold

[2] F. Ray Marshall, *Labor in the South* (Cambridge: Harvard University Press, 1967).

[3] August Meier and Elliott Rudwick, *From Plantation to Ghetto* (New York: Hill and Wang, 1966), p. 158.

[4] *Ibid.* If this membership figure is correct, the CFACU would have been the largest black organization in U.S. history. Unfortunately, as Meier and Rudwick point out, there is very little available information about the CFACU.

[5] *Ibid.*

[6] *Ibid.*

as to challenge racism openly in favor of common cooperative action by all workers and farmers.[7] The cooperatives established by these groups were short-lived, however, and eventually failed. The political programs of the Knights of Labor, the Farmer's Alliance, the CFACU, and the Populists were opposed by conservative Democratic leaders because these groups threatened to split the white vote and give greater political power to blacks. The Populists' cooperative programs also were opposed by conservatives as being socialistic and undermining the free enterprise system.

Other important reasons for the failure of the coops established by these organizations were undercapitalization, overexpansion, and poor management.

The Farmers Educational and Cooperative Union of America, founded in Raines County, Texas, in 1902, had as one of its objectives the creation of buying and credit cooperatives for poor farmers, but like the Farmers Alliance its membership was restricted to whites. Most of the coops it established did not survive, frequently because of poor management; where they succeeded, they were transformed into private corporations.[8]

The most significant attempt, prior to current efforts, to establish coops among poor farmers in the South occurred during the New Deal period. The Farm Security Administration (FSA), a federal agency instituted in 1937, operated a special series of programs designed to help small low-income farmers and was responsible for the formation of 25,543 poor people's cooperatives.[9] Although official FSA policy was to encourage poor farmers to join existing cooperatives, where this was not possible FSA extended cooperative grant and loan funds to lease land; to establish buying and marketing associations; to purchase farm machinery, breeding stock, veterinary services, and insurance; and to obtain water and other facilities.

---

[7] Marshall, *Labor in the South*, p. 89.

[8] *Ibid.*, p. 92.

[9] Sidney Baldwin, *Poverty and Politics* (Chapel Hill: University of North Carolina Press, 1968), p. 203.

Although the FSA's local marketing and supply enterprises were more numerous, the land leasing associations and collective farms were more ambitious and controversial. These coops were designed to improve the tenure status of poor farmers by enabling them to lease large tracts of land, which in turn were divided and subleased as family farms to the individual members. This type of co-op was used rather extensively in the plantation areas of the South. For example, in 1939 the FSA arranged for 827 families to lease seventeen cotton plantations in Arkansas, Mississippi, and Louisiana. By 1943, fifty-two FSA-sponsored coops had a total of 136,368 acres, much of which was concentrated in the deep South.[10]

Some of these cooperative settlements were all black. For example, in 1934 the FSA purchased a 12,000-acre plantation in Gee's Bend (Wilcox County), Alabama, to resettle one hundred destitute black families. FSA also provided loan funds for housing, farm equipment, supplies, and community improvements. This was one of FSA's most successful experiments. Not only did its efforts result in improved farming, but they also yielded better nutrition, health, housing, and education.[11]

Another coop settlement was in Holmes County, Mississippi, in 1941, when FSA assisted one hundred black farm families in acquiring seventeen acres of land, establishing a cooperative cotton gin and a cooperative grocery store, and constructing several rent houses.

According to one report, some of these settlements had blacks and whites working together on equal terms.[12] But wherever they were established, they met strong opposition from racist politicians and other white community leaders.

The collective farms were the most unconventional of the FSA coops. They actually were "cooperative corporations" governed by elected boards of directors. The members were employed by the

[10] *Ibid.*, p. 206.

[11] Wilma Dykeman and James Stokely, *Seeds of Southern Change* (Chicago: University of Chicago Press, 1962).

[12] Gunnar Myrdal, *An American Dilemma* (New York: Harper & Bros., 1944), p. 276.

association, worked under foremen selected by the managers, and were paid on the basis of prevailing wages for hired farm workers.[13]

As noted earlier, collective farms rarely have been successful because the divisive influences of individual differences make such collective undertakings difficult, even under the most favorable circumstances. And circumstances for the FSA experiments were far from favorable. They came at a time when there were heavy population pressures on the land. Furthermore, according to a United Nations' agricultural cooperative survey,

the families themselves had next to no capital, and they were not very capable farmers. Government funds were available at low cost and also much technical and administrative help. But no very great improvement in farming requiring complex machinery or much capital investment could be undertaken with full confidence. Neither markets for produce, nor alternative employment for workers, were well assured. The prospective members of the collectives were not sentimentally attached to particular plots of available lands, nor were they in cohesive social groups, despite the economic adversity they had suffered. They lacked "cooperative spirit."[14]

Hundreds of thousands of poor people in the rural South received valuable assistance from the FSA and other New Deal antipoverty programs. As we have already indicated, blacks shared in these benefits, but not as much as they could or should have because the FSA programs were too limited in view of the size of the problem and were administered in a discriminatory manner.[15] During the 1930s and 1940s, as now, a disproportionate share of agricultural benefit payments went to big landlords. In essence, small farmers in general and black farmers in particular lacked the political and economic power to protect their interests.[16]

The problem of discrimination in the FSA does not seem to have been due as much to racist policies as to the structure of its programs and the attitudes of its local personnel. Indeed, several top-ranking FSA officials fought persistently against racial discrimi-

[13] *Ibid.*
[14] United Nations, *Rural Progress through Cooperatives,* p. 81–82.
[15] *Ibid.*
[16] Myrdal, *An American Dilemma,* pp. 274–75.

nation and openly criticized discriminatory actions in several of the FSA's official publications.[17] But because the FSA did not have adequate control over the local administration of its projects, the special committees of local farmers which screened applications for assistance discriminated against blacks. These overtly discriminatory acts by individuals at the local level were reinforced by a more subtle form of "indirect discrimination" which was inherent in the FSA programs. Many poor blacks were unable to obtain assistance because FSA programs "creamed."

County supervisors tended to become preoccupied with making a good showing in their loan collection records, to seek escape from the local agriculturalists' suggestion that the FSA was wasting its time with the dregs of rural society, and to simplify their tasks. They, therefore, tended to select loan borrowers from higher social and economic levels—applicants with larger farming units, higher net incomes, greater net worth, fewer dependent children, better health, and more education. In other words, many of the FSA supervisors were working with the upper crust of the low-income farm population.[18]

It must have been obvious that such an approach would limit the ability of poor blacks to obtain a fair share of FSA benefits. Moreover, the fact that blacks had a better repayment record than whites, despite the fact that their gross cash incomes were 40 percent lower than those of white borrowers, suggests that blacks were much more cautiously selected than whites.[19]

One evaluation of FSA cooperative development programs concluded that they involved relatively few blacks. In 1940, for example, there were less than two thousand black families in FSA cooperatives and settlement programs.[20]

Although some of the FSA coops, particularly the smaller and more informal ones, had a rather high failure rate because of insufficient volume, poor patronage, and management difficulties,

[17] *Ibid.*, p. 274.

[18] Baldwin, *Poverty and Politics*, p. 218.

[19] Richard Sterner and Associates, *The Negroes' Share* (New York: Harper, 1943), p. 191.

[20] *Ibid.*

their rate of failure was no greater than that of private manufacturing enterprises.[21]

The failure rate among FSA coops increased slightly between 1943 and 1946, but by the end of June 1946, 84 percent of the 25,543 cooperatives which had been established with FSA funds were still in operation, and more than half, 63 percent, of the loans had been completely repaid.[22] Many of these coops became viable enterprises.

Opposition from the agricultural establishment (the USDA extension service, state extension services, state land grant agricultural colleges, county agents, southern congressmen, private farm machinery and supply companies, established cooperatives, and especially the American Farm Bureau Federation), which considered the New Deal antipoverty programs a threat to their economic and political power base, caused congressional opposition to the FSA, leading to a series of crippling restrictions beginning in 1943. In 1946 the FSA was replaced by the Farmers Home Administration (FHA).

Although very limited information is available that would permit an evaluation of black coops in the rural South during the 1930s and 1940s, a 1950 study by Nathan A. Pitts gives some insight into the causes of their success or failure.[23] The earliest coops among Negroes in North Carolina were informal credit unions established in 1929. By 1948, however, almost a hundred credit unions and at least forty-eight other cooperatives (nine consumer stores, thirty-two machinery coops, four curb markets, two health associations, and one housing project) had been organized among blacks.

Only one of these coops, the Orange County Credit Union at Chapel Hill, had a racially mixed membership. The Excelsior Credit Union, formed by twenty blacks with $193.75 at Gastonia in 1942,

[21] James G. Maddox, "The Farm Security Administration" (Ph.D. diss., Harvard University, 1950), p. 292.

[22] *Ibid.*

[23] Nathan Alvin Pitts, *The Cooperative Movement in Negro Communities in North Carolina* (Washington: The Catholic University of America Press, 1950).

35

rejected membership applications from whites. These coops were all-black primarily because racial solidarity was one of the unifying principles upon which they were organized. In addition, most whites strongly opposed racially integrated coops. In 1947, for example, a mob of about two hundred whites drove an integrated group out of Tyrrel County. This group was sponsored by the Fellowship of Southern Churchmen and was constructing a new cooperative building.

The North Carolina cooperatives were instigated mainly by ministers, teachers, or county agents. The earliest organizations seem to have been credit unions formed because of the strategic importance of credit in economic improvement. Other coops often were encouraged by credit unions. Education also played a role in the activities of these associations, which often were organized around, or stimulated by, schools. The centers of cooperative activity among blacks in North Carolina during this period, for instance, seem to have been the Bricks Rural Life School at Bricks and the Tyrrel County Training School.

The credit unions also seem to have been the most successful of the North Carolina coops, apparently because they were supported by federal legislation and statewide associations which provide simple model organizational structures and procedures that were easily understood by people with limited education and experiences. Some of these credit unions became economically viable organizations and are still in existence today. For example, in 1969 the Excelsior Credit Union, discussed earlier, had more than 3,000 members; real estate holdings of $68,231; $94,913 in other investments; and had loans totaling more than one million dollars. The Chowan County Credit Union, founded in Edenton in 1941, had 1,800 members in 1969; assets of $270,000; and $212,000 in loans. By 1969 the Pasquotonk County Credit Union, organized at Elizabeth City in 1944, had 322 members; assets of $28,410.50; and loans of $395,394.74. The Gates County Credit Union, established in 1945 at Gatesville, had 374 members and assets of $49,591.82 in 1969 when its loans totaled $42,335.67.[24]

[24] Reports of the North Carolina Foundation for Rural Development, 1969.

The other types of coops studied by Pitts seemed to have been relatively fragile undertakings, highly dependent on key individual leaders, and often collapsing when these leaders were no longer available.

A study of black low-income coops in Alabama during this period found patterns very similar to those reported by Pitts for North Carolina.[25]

EMERGENCE OF THE NEW POOR PEOPLE'S COOPERATIVE MOVEMENT

The rapid growth of cooperatives among poor blacks in the rural South during the 1960s was an outgrowth of the intensive civil rights activities in the region during that period. The civil rights movement aroused nationwide concern for the plight of poor disenfranchised black farmers and created the pride, confidence, and cohesiveness in black communities which stimulated self-help efforts. Many of the coops were organized by field staff workers of the various civil rights organizations, particularly the Student Nonviolent Coordinating Committee (SNCC), the Southern Christian Leadership Conference (SCLC), and the Congress of Racial Equality (CORE).

In addition, a number of Catholic and Protestant religious leaders were actively involved in the promotion of poor people's cooperatives in the rural South during those years. For example, the Reverend Francis X. Walter, Director of the Selma Inter-Religious Project, was a founder of the Freedom Quilting Bee in Gee's Bend, Alabama, and actively supported the Southwest Alabama Farmers Cooperative Association (SWAFCA), which is discussed below. The Delta Ministry, a group of Mississippi clergymen sponsored by the National Council of Churches, established "Freedom City," a 400-acre cooperative community for evicted farm workers near Wayside. The Delta Ministry also helped other Mississippi low-income coops.[26]

[25] M. B. Lightfoote, "An Economic Analysis of Specified Incorporated and Unincorporated Cooperative Associations Operated by Negro Farmers in Alabama" (M.A. thesis, Tuskegee Institute, 1953).

[26] Ralph Galt, "The New Cooperative Movement among Low-Income People in Four Southern States" (mimeographed, August 1968).

Other organizations which played an important role in the establishment of the new cooperatives were the National Sharecroppers Fund (NSF), the Southern Regional Council,[27] the Cooperative League of the U.S.A., and the Credit Unions National Association (CUNA).

Very few of the established coops in the South have helped the new coops. Although the Cotton Producers Coop in Atlanta furnished fertilizer to SWAFCA when other distributors refused,[28] most of the older cooperatives in the South are hostile to the new movement. The established coop at Selma, Alabama, refused membership to blacks and would sell nothing to SWAFCA. In Greenwood, Mississippi, the Farmers' Coop refused to employ blacks and therefore was boycotted by the civil rights groups. The Banks for Cooperatives, a financial organization owned by a group of established cooperatives, also has refused to help the poor people's coops.

A number of private foundations have given financial support to the new coops, however. The Ford Foundation has been the major source of private support for poor people's coops in the South. Other foundations that have helped the new organizations include the Field Foundation, the New York Foundation, and the Aaron Norman Foundation. A number of smaller foundations have formed the Cooperative Assistance Fund, a consortium which has provided help to the coops. The Episcopal Church, the Methodist Church, and the Presbyterian Church have also provided some financial assistance.

Various government agencies have helped the coops, especially the Office of Economic Opportunity, which has been the main source of financial assistance to the new organizations. Under the Economic Opportunity Act of 1964, the Farmers Home Administration (FHA) administers a low-interest (4-⅛ percent) loan pro-

[27] Al Ulmer, "Cooperatives, Credit Unions and Poor People," *Special Report* (Atlanta, Ga.: The Southern Regional Council, 1966), and "Cooperatives, Credit Unions, and Poor People—a Second Look," *Special Report* (Atlanta, Ga.: The Southern Regional Council, 1968).

[28] Galt, "The New Cooperative Movement."

gram to help coops with limited resources, although they have not been as helpful as they could and should have been because of racial discrimination; inadequate appropriations; political opposition to loans and grants to controversial coops; red tape (which coop leaders suspect is often deliberately used by hostile FHA administrators to frustrate the new coops' chances for success) which delays the approval and disbursement of funds past the time for their strategic use in the agricultural cycle; and inadequate supervision of loans and grants by OEO and FHA.

The activities of these organizations and agencies will be discussed at greater length in the following chapters.

SOUTHERN CONSUMERS, THE SOUTHERN COOPERATIVE DEVELOPMENT PROGRAM, AND THE FEDERATION OF SOUTHERN COOPERATIVES

Father A. J. McKnight, a black Catholic priest in rural Louisiana, was one of the main initiators of the new cooperative movement among the rural poor. Like many others, Father McKnight arrived at the cooperative idea for the rural poor after first having failed with other antipoverty approaches. Because 75 percent of the blacks in Vermillion Parish, Louisiana, were illiterate when he came there in 1957, Father McKnight initially attempted to teach people to read and write. After two years, he decided that the self-improvement program had failed because very poor black people suffered from a "poverty of the spirit worse than that of the body." As a consequence, there was little interest in the literacy classes. He therefore decided that coops might generate hope and self-esteem as well as produce economic benefits. During the summer of 1960 he studied cooperative philosophy at St. Francis University in Nova Scotia, where the Antigonish movement had been very successful in using coops for social and economic purposes. After returning to Louisiana in 1961, Father McKnight formed the Southern Consumers Education Foundation (SCEF), a nonprofit organization for general and cooperative education, and the Southern Consumers Cooperative, a multipurpose economic development organization. After the cooperatives were formed, Father McKnight centered educational programs around cooperative activities and therefore had much greater participation from the poor, who now had greater incentives to learn.

Elsewhere in the South, civil rights activists also were attracted by the cooperative idea. In Black Belt agricultural areas, acreage restrictions and increasing capital requirements made it difficult for small farmers to compete. As noted earlier, many displaced operators became agricultural laborers, but others, encouraged by civil rights activists and federal antipoverty programs, attempted to meet these capital requirements through individual or cooperative loans or grants from the Office of Economic Opportunity and the FHA. It was hoped that cooperatives would make it possible for small farmers to purchase and use the latest machinery, reduce farm costs, improve productivity, market agricultural products, supplement incomes through handicraft production or small-scale industry, provide consumer education and credit unions for loans and savings facilities, buy land, and generally engage in self-improvement activities. As will be seen later, however, cooperatives were not restricted to agriculture, and indeed some have been organized in urban areas.

Because the promoters of cooperatives knew small farmers would not be able to continue producing cotton unless they pooled their resources and efforts and acquired machinery, they hoped to diversify their activities and turn to labor-intensive vegetable and livestock production.

The cooperatives formed by poor blacks during the 1960s usually were organized around churches or civil rights groups in the rural areas, but some were handicraft or consumers' coops in urban areas.

The real beginnings of what may be called a "movement" among poor people's cooperatives came in the summer of 1966, when several organizers and members of low-income coops met with representatives from the Southern Regional Council, the Cooperative League, the U.S. Office of Economic Opportunity, the National Sharecroppers Fund, the Credit Unions National Association, and other groups at the Mount Beulah Conference Center near Edwards, Mississippi, to exchange ideas and experiences concerning cooperatives for the rural poor. A special continuation committee was appointed to develop a proposal for a cooperative demonstration project, solicit the funds necessary to put it into operation, and make plans for the formation of a federation of poor people's cooperatives. As a result of these activities, in June 1967 the Ford Foundation funded the Southern Cooperative Development Program (SCDP) through the Southern Consumers Education Foundation.

THE SOUTHERN COOPERATIVE DEVELOPMENT PROGRAM

The Ford grant of $578,000 to the SCDP was designed to demonstrate the feasibility of poor people's cooperatives by concentrating its efforts in Louisiana, Mississippi, Alabama, and part of Tennessee.

SCDP's main objectives were to: (1) assist established low-income cooperatives in obtaining credit and technical assistance; and (2) to promote the development of new cooperatives by providing training in community organization techniques and cooperative principles.

The SCDP carried out its activities through twenty-four field representatives under the direction of Father McKnight and John Zippert, a twenty-three-year-old white civil rights activist from New York, who were responsible to SCEF's Board of Directors. In addition, an advisory committee was established to review accomplishments, assess programs, and screen and recommend candidates for staff positions.

SCDP initially planned to organize many new cooperatives in its four-state area but soon decided to concentrate on existing cooperatives in eighteen communities. SCDP leaders were aware of the "demonstration effect" that successful enterprises would have in promoting the cooperative idea among poor people as well as the frustration and despair that would result from another failure after hopes had been raised. Indeed, skepticism, born of many unsuccessful movements, is a major obstacle to self-help activities among the rural poor in the South. The SCDP, therefore, decided to concentrate its efforts on about twenty-five cooperatives and credit unions. The Cooperative Development Program's activities are described in chapter 4.

THE FEDERATION OF SOUTHERN COOPERATIVES

In February 1967 representatives from twenty-two low-income cooperatives, most of which were affiliated with the SCDP, met in Atlanta, established the Federation of Southern Cooperatives (FSC), and selected Charles Prejean, who also was a close associate of Father McKnight in Louisiana, as president. Prejean subsequently became the first executive director of the FSC.

The Federation is open to any cooperative in the seventeen states in which it operates, and is governed by a board of directors which consists of one representative from each of the states in which the Federation has a member. The Federation is financed by federal grants, annual dues from members ($1.00 per person per year), and contributions from foundations and individuals.

The services of the SCDP and FSC (which merged into one organization in the spring of 1970) are very important because of the numerous problems confronting the new, predominantly black, limited-resource cooperatives in the South. The following chapters contain analytical descriptions of several of the new poor people's coops which show their general nature and the various types of assistance they have received from the SCDP and the Federation.

4

A Profile of the New Poor People's Cooperatives

Several different types of rural poor people's cooperatives have been formed in the South. These include organizations to purchase supplies for farm and household use; to market vegetables, livestock, and other farm products; to purchase machinery; to produce and market handicrafts and garments; to provide a source of credit and to hold savings; to buy land; to catch and market fish; and to provide housing. Table 2 shows the geographical distribution of FSC coops and coop membership by type.

AGRICULTURAL MARKETING AND SUPPLY COOPS

Our sample includes twenty-four, predominantly black, low-income agricultural coops which had a combined membership of approximately 5,900 small farmers in the summer of 1969.

The largest low-income agricultural marketing and supply cooperative in the South is the South West Alabama Farmers Cooperative Association (SWAFCA), located in Selma. SWAFCA is composed of 1,800 poor farm families, all of whom are black and who reside in ten contiguous central and western Alabama Black

Table 2. New Low-Income Cooperatives Affiliated with the Federation of Southern Cooperatives, August 1969

Location	Agricultural Marketing and Supply		Credit Unions		Handicrafts and Small Industry		Consumers		Fishing		Others		Total	
	Coops	Members	Coops	Members	Coops	Members	Coops	Members	Coops	Members	Coops	Members	Coops	Members
Alabama	2	1,825	6	2,784	2	108	3	230	—	—	2	2,451	14	7,379*
Arkansas	1	300	1	150	—	—	2	80	—	—	—	—	4	530
Florida	4	384	1	101	—	—	—	—	1	92	—	—	6	577
Georgia	2	400	1	190	1	55	3	490	—	—	2	—	9	
Kentucky	1	10	—	—	2	55	—	—	—	—	—	—	3	65
Louisiana	3	290	4	1,833	—	—	—	—	—	—	1	2,050	8	4,173
Mississippi	5	1,875	1	500+	4	960	3	1,080	1	25	3	497	17	4,937
Missouri	1	200	—	—	1	46	—	—	—	—	—	—	2	200
North Carolina	1	175	—	—	1	150	—	—	—	—	—	—	2	325
South Carolina	3	224	2	400	—	—	1	—	1	10	1	80	8	714
Tennessee	—	—	—	—	1	25	2	1,300	—	—	—	—	3	1,325
Texas	—	—	—	—	1	35	1	200	—	—	—	—	2	235
Virginia	1	300	—	—	—	—	—	—	—	—	—	—	1	300
West Virginia	—	—	—	—	1	30	—	—	—	—	—	—	1	30
Total	24	5,982	16	5,918	14	1,474	15	3,030	3	127	8	2,702	80	

* Membership totals are slightly inflated because some members belong to more than one coop.
Source: Federation of Southern Cooperatives.

Belt counties (Choctaw, Dallas, Green, Hale, Lowndes, Marengo, Monroe, Perry, Sumpter, and Wilcox).

In 1960 the population of these ten counties was 229,000, of which 148,000 were black. All but one of these counties (Dallas) were among the three hundred lowest income counties in the nation, and three (Green, Lowndes, and Perry) had median family incomes below $1,000. By 1965 none of the ten counties had per capita income as high as that for the state as a whole ($1,920), and six (Green, Hale, Lowndes, Perry, Sumpter, and Wilcox) ranked among the one hundred lowest income counties in per capita income in the United States. Four of the counties (Green, Hale, Lowndes, and Perry) had per capita incomes of less than $1,000. Green County, with a per capita income of $849, was the lowest.[1] When SWAFCA was formed, 40 percent of its members farmed with mules, and 38 percent had only hand tools, mainly hoes.

SWAFCA was an outgrowth of the voter registration drives undertaken in the Black Belt during 1964 and 1965 and the famous Selma-to-Montgomery "March for Freedom." The Association's early promoters were Albert Turner of the Southern Christian Leadership Conference; Shirley Mesher, an independent civil rights worker from Washington; and Lewis Black, a former school teacher in rural Alabama who became a member of the field staff of the Federation of Southern Cooperatives. Additional support and assistance was provided by the National Sharecroppers Fund, the Southern Regional Council, and the Cooperative League of the U.S.A.

SWAFCA's main objective was to enable its members to supplement their meager earnings from cotton by producing vegetables and marketing them cooperatively. The coop also helps its members to economize on the purchase of supplies and provides technical assistance in the production of vegetables, especially peas, cucumbers, and okra. It was felt that diversification would raise the incomes per acre of poor farmers and make them less vulnerable to fluctuations in incomes from cotton.

[1] U.S. Bureau of the Census, *Current Population Survey,* 1960.

A fall in cotton prices, mechanization, and reprisals for civil rights activities, together with unsuccessful attempts to get the aid of federal and state agricultural agencies in shifting from cotton to vegetable production, caused a group of seven hundred black farmers in this area to feel the need to pool their resources and help themselves. These farmers were, therefore, discussing the formation of some kind of organization when the civil rights workers started organizing coops in December 1966. On March 22, 1967, when the group numbered about eight hundred, SWAFCA was formally incorporated in Dallas County, Alabama.

SWAFCA's organizational structure is simple and typical of the other new poor people's cooperatives. Its board consisted of two elected members from each county. The president of the board and other officers (one or more vice presidents, a recording secretary, a corresponding secretary, a financial secretary, and a treasurer) were elected by the board. The board and its executive committee are responsible for general supervision and control and have the authority to formulate policy and to employ and dismiss employees. In addition, each of the ten counties has its own local board to make decisions concerning cooperative affairs in each county.

Although SWAFCA's annual membership fee is $1.00, it has raised an insignificant amount (less than 1 percent) of its capital from this source. The coop's main sources of funds have been a loan of $25,000 from the International Foundation for Independence (IFI) in Exeter, New Hampshire; a loan of $5,000 from Operation Freedom in Philadelphia; three grants totaling $1,336,-510 from the U.S. Office of Economic Opportunity (OEO); a grant of $87,000 from the Economic Development Administration (EDA); and a loan of $3,100 from the Southern Cooperative Development Program.

With the initial loan from the IFI, the coop purchased seed, fertilizer, and other supplies which it sold to the members on credit. The loan from Operation Freedom was for operating capital. The OEO grants enabled SWAFCA to hire administrative and technical staff (manager, assistant manager, comptroller, horticulturalist, marketing specialist, education specialist, field supervisors, administrative assistant, secretaries, and clerk-typist), establish a $35,000 loan guarantee fund, which was used to secure another $273,000 of credit and to defray general operating expenses. The $854,000 loan obtained from the Farmers Home Administration, after considerable conflict with the state and federal leaders of that organization, was used to construct receiving and distribution sheds in each of the ten counties and to expand the revolving loan fund. The EDA grant financed feasibility studies on expansion possibilities.

During the first nine months of 1967, SWAFCA marketed over a million pounds of peas, okra, cucumbers, and cotton for 850 members, grossed $107,000, and had an operating loss of less than $1,000. When the initial OEO grant was received in October 1967, membership had risen to about 1,500. In 1968, despite a drought and serious internal difficulties, SWAFCA handled produce for nearly 2,000 members.

SWAFCA has been plagued by a host of problems which have limited its effectiveness. Some of these problems are due to harrassment from white racist politicians and business leaders, and others are due to poor management and inadequate membership support. When SWAFCA was started, local supply companies refused to sell fertilizer and lime to its members, process plants curtailed purchases of peas and cucumbers from them, truck drivers transporting the coop's produce were intimidated, eight white families among the original members of the coop were ostracized by local whites and finally withdrew, and the organization was attacked by local newspapers.

SWAFCA's efforts to obtain federal grants also met strong opposition. When the coop's first OEO grant was announced, the Association's enemies (a group of local politicians including mayors and probate judges from each of the ten counties and representatives of two large pickle companies) led by the mayor of Selma organized a special committee which, with the six members of the Alabama congressional delegation, met with OEO officials in Washington and charged that SWAFCA was a communist-inspired black power organization. This group also demanded a complete investigation of the coop by the Federal Bureau of Investigation. On June 8, 1967, Alabama Governor Lurleen Wallace vetoed SWAFCA's OEO grant, but her veto was overridden by OEO Director Sergeant Shriver after an FBI investigation.

The harassment continued, however. The Alabama legislature passed a joint resolution asking OEO to reverse its action because the grant would be used "to finance the lawless Black Panther movement designed to overthrow the government of their country and particularly the government of the Southern states." SWAFCA's second OEO grant also was vetoed by Lurleen Wallace's successor, Governor Albert Brewer. When his veto was overridden by OEO, Selma Mayor Joe Smitherman obtained a state court order blocking the use of all federal funds by the coop on the grounds of malfeasance and other charges. At OEO's request, the U.S. Department of Justice intervened on SWAFCA's behalf and filed countersuits. As a result, the state court order was lifted by the U.S. District Court in Mobile, which issued a temporary restraining order against Smitherman, Governor Brewer, and Dallas County Circuit Court Judge James A. Hare.

SWAFCA's management problems have stemmed from the shortage of competent and dedicated administrative specialists on its staff and board of directors. The coop's first manager, a wealthy local black businessman, performed very poorly and did not devote sufficient time to his job. The evidence of poor management included: failure of the manager to attend board meetings, to hire staff, obtain essential equipment in time and train members to use it; delays in getting seed, fertilizer, and pesticides, which caused late plantings, reduced acreages, and prevented the planting of different seed varieties; delays in the construction of equipment and grading sheds; and failure to make contractual arrangements for substandard produce crops which were still useable.

The management problem was further complicated by the inexperience of SWAFCA's Board of Directors and conflicts within the organization. Internal disunity resulted from personality conflicts and poor grass-roots organization. SWAFCA's members had very limited understanding of cooperative principles. As a result, some SWAFCA members sold only part of their crops to SWAFCA and the rest to the Association's competitors.

SWAFCA made some progress during 1969 but not enough to ensure the organization's survival as a viable economic enterprise. The indifferent manager was discharged. The new manager was younger and had less business experience but seemed to be aware of the problems confronting the organization, especially the need to overcome its structural problems in order to make maximum use of the available resources. In addition to his other problems, the new manager had to assume all marketing responsibilities when the coop's marketing specialist, a white southerner, resigned.

SWAFCA's volume dropped by about 24 percent (purchased from about 1,250 members) in 1969. Net proceeds increased, however, because of significant improvements in grading, quality control, and marketing. These improvements are especially significant in view of the fact that SWAFCA did not have a marketing specialist most of that year.

SWAFCA's decline in volume during 1969 resulted from a variety of causes. Although political factors were involved, some of its members defected because they disapproved of SWAFCA's practice, later changed, of paying for produce weekly rather than daily, as most members preferred, and were dissatisfied with SWAFCA's inadequate facilities.

The SCDP and the Federation helped SWAFCA overcome internal disunity, educate the board, expand membership and increase its loyalty to the coop, and improve its technical and marketing efficiency. Both organizations made short-term loans to SWAFCA for emergency operating capital and sponsored management training seminars for the coop's staff and board of directors. The SCDP assigned three of its full-time field representatives to work in the area, and in the spring of 1969, the Federation assigned its entire field staff of thirteen to work in an intensive month-long membership education and recruitment drive for SWAFCA.

In addition, the SCDP made a loan of $5,500 to help twelve evicted farmers buy 301 acres of farm land in Dallas County, and both the SCDP and the Federation made loans ($25,000 and $10,000 respectively) to help settle perhaps forty families on 901 acres in Sumpter County. All of these families became members of SWAFCA.

In spite of its mistakes, failures, and uncertain future in 1970, this coop has made some real progress—although it has been slow and at considerable cost. Its accomplishments include:

1) SWAFCA has undoubtedly improved its members' net real income by raising the prices they received and lowering the cost of supplies. Moreover, the economic position of SWAFCA's members is more secure because of greater diversification.

2) SWAFCA's leaders have gone through a learning period which should put them in a much better position to make progress in the future. Many past mistakes are being corrected. In 1970 its leaders were improving production procedures and methods of storing and transporting produce to market. Although there is still some distrust of whites and outsiders, in the spring of 1970 four whites were on its senior technical staff.

3) There is also some evidence that SWAFCA has had an impact on the USDA and other institutions with which it must deal. SWAFCA's conflict with FHA over funding caused that agency to adopt new procedures for making loans by recognizing demonstration projects. Moreover, FHA now permits SWAFCA to vouch for loans to its members, whose limited assets previously made them ineligible for loans. In the spring of 1970, 110 of SWAFCA's members were beneficiaries of this loan arrangement. Other government agencies and local merchants are more willing to deal with the Association. County agents have started inviting SWAFCA representatives to grower-buyer meetings where agricultural marketing opportunities are discussed. These forms of recognition undoubtedly will serve to strengthen SWAFCA's support in the local community. In addition, there can be little question that SWAFCA has had an impact on the local political structure by providing greater economic independence. SWAFCA members

have been elected to such political offices as county commissioner, school board, justice of the peace, and various municipal positions.

Because of its size and the attention it has received from friend and foe alike, SWAFCA's success or failure will have a profound impact on coops among poor farmers throughout the South. If it is successful in overcoming its problems, it will strengthen and expand its membership in the area and cause the idea of cooperation to spread. On the other hand, if it grows weaker, it will lose support from its own members and will deal a severe blow to the cooperative idea. SWAFCA provides a good test case because any cooperative which could overcome all of the problems facing SWAFCA could succeed anywhere.

The Grand Marie Vegetable Producers Cooperative, Inc., with four hundred members in five Louisiana parishes (St. Landry, St. Martin, Acadia, Lafayette, and Evangeline), was organized at Sunset, Louisiana, in the fall of 1965 by a group of poor black farmers who felt that they were being exploited by local white produce brokers. Prior to the formation of the coop, these farmers were at the mercy of local shippers, who paid as little as 75 cents per crate for their sweet potatoes, and several of whom had refused to purchase produce from persons involved in civil rights activities.

These experiences caused a group of small farmers to form their own marketing association. With the assistance of Father McKnight, they secured a $50,000 grant from the Office of Economic Opportunity and inaugurated and intensive drive, directed by Charles Prejean and John Zippert, to recruit and educate potential members.

Grand Marie's initial financing was a $68,000 FHA loan used to hire staff and to purchase processing equipment and a storage shed. The manager's salary was paid with the SCDP grant.

Grand Marie had been in operation for three years in the summer of 1969. During its first season, the organization marketed 40,000 crates of sweet potatoes, purchased from its members at

$1.25 per crate, forcing the local shippers to raise their prices to that level. However, the coop had a first year operating loss of about $30,000 because of spoilage problems, poor grading, high labor costs, poor accounting procedures, and an unpaid bill of $7,000.

By the beginning of the second harvest season, Grand Marie's operating funds were exhausted, and it was unable to pay its members cash upon delivery. As a result, the number of farmers selling to the coop dwindled from 200 to less than 75, and Grand Marie's volume dropped by 16,000 crates. Estimates of the coop's second year operating loss range up to $29,000. However, despite these difficulties, the coop expanded its activities to include the marketing of okra, cabbage, onions, cucumbers, peppers, and other vegetables. Grand Marie sold more than 200 tons of fertilizer to its members in the spring of 1969 for a net profit of $1,000.

By the spring of 1970, most of Grand Marie's problems resulted from management and financial difficulties. The organization's manager was dedicated but inexperienced, and the board, composed entirely of poor farmers, had not yet developed the capacity to function effectively. Grand Marie also has experienced serious marketing problems, which resulted in some costly losses on accounts receivable.

In order to help Grand Marie solve its problems, the SCDP assigned three of its organizers to help the Association regain dissident members and to recruit new ones. In addition, in 1968 the SCDP provided management training for Grand Marie and hired an experienced black produce broker to handle the organization's sales. The Federation helped Grand Marie through loans and management training and aided this coop to secure a $50,000 emergency operating loan from a Providence, Rhode Island, millionaire.

As a result of these measures, Grand Marie marketed 62,000 crates of sweet potatoes in 1969 and cut its operating loss for the year to about $16,000. However, if an account receivable of $20,-000 is not collected, the loss will increase to $36,000.

Although Grand Marie claims four hundred members, less than half that number paid membership fees in the summer of 1969.

Most of the farmers in the coop's vicinity were poor tenants or sharecroppers, and cooperation is a new experience for them. Moreover, because of the coop's many problems, it has not been adequately able to service its membership and to pay them promptly for their produce. Very few members attended monthly meetings, and the coop's affairs were therefore dominated by a few active board members. SCDP organizers helped to educate the members and to strengthen their participation in and control of the organization.

Like SWAFCA, Grand Marie has encountered strong opposition and harassment from local white politicians and competition from a rival, predominantly white, cooperative. This competing organization, which was also financed by FHA, is controlled by a local white sweet potato farmer, who was a member of Grand Marie's organizing committee. However, the rival coop leader and about twenty whites withdrew their support from Grand Marie when he was not selected as manager and because the coop refused to purchase an inoperative canning plant (owned by a friend of his) after a feasibility study undertaken by USDA officials from Washington disclosed that the plant was too dilapidated to be eligible for federal loan funds.

Although blacks comprise more than two-thirds of the membership of Grand Marie's rival, a few white members were in firm control in 1969. One black farmer was on the coop's eight-man board of directors, but he became inactive in late 1969.

The West Batesville Farmers Cooperative (WBFC), located in Panola County, Mississippi, provides custom harvesting, combining, and marketing services for 265 members. The WBFC was organized in the spring of 1965 by SNCC field workers, a representative of the National Sharecroppers Fund, and a group of small farmers.

WBFC was formed to eliminate what was perceived to be exploitation by a white okra buyer. Prior to the establishment of the coop, this purchaser bought (for 4 cents per pound) virtually all of the okra produced by the area's black farmers. After an attempt to negotiate higher prices from the broker failed, the black farmers decided to form a coop. Because it was too late to secure contracts from okra buyers and processing plants, these farmers had to sell on the open market in Memphis, where prices fluctuated from day to day. For the first two months, the coop was able to pay 5 cents per pound to its patrons, but near the end of the summer, the price was reduced to 4 cents per pound, and some of the members went back to the white okra buyer.

WBFC was chartered in the fall of 1965 and obtained a $114,-000 loan from the FHA, which was used to purchase three automatic cotton pickers, three combines, four trucks, and other equipment. This machinery was acquired to offset the effect of a federal court ruling which created a labor shortage because it ended the practice of dismissing classes for black children during the cotton harvest season.

The coop completed its fourth season in 1969 and was beset by a number of serious problems. The organization had lost money every year, was deeply in debt, and had not been able to make full payments on its FHA loan. The financial difficulties resulted from bad weather and poor cotton harvests, poor record-keeping practices, bad management, the purchase of machinery that was inadequate for the intended purposes and improperly used, and insufficient membership patronage.

Although WBFC lost money on its equipment in 1969, the coop was successful in marketing okra and peas and in providing a new source of income for many of its member farmers. Indeed, WBFC's contracts with the Birdseye Frozen Food Company for these crops were large enough to permit it to share its contract with the Mileston Coop in Holmes County, Mississippi.

Moreover, WBFC seems to be overcoming its management, marketing, record-keeping and financial problems. The SCDP and the Federation provided the coop with management and marketing help, and the SCDP assigned a full-time field organizer to work with the coop. Records were put in good condition as a result of help from the Mississippi Federated Coop and the Mississippi Extension Service. WBFC also seemingly has had good support from local USDA agencies.

In 1968 WBFC obtained a grant of approximately $100,000 from OEO to help overcome its financial problems and to employ a full-time manager and secretary. The coop also overcame its initial difficulties in improperly using the machinery and late in 1969 was meeting its FHA payments.

With better management and machinery, West Batesville should improve its members' cotton and bean productivity on the more than 3,000 black-owned acres, which had previously been harvested by hand. Moreover, the coop has facilitated diversification into vegetables, especially okra and soybeans. In 1968, 114 of WBFC's members had an average of between seventy and eighty acres in soybeans as a result of the equipment purchases. The advantages of mechanization and improved production and marketing techniques would not have been available to West Batesville's members without the coop.

Although the WBFC is far from being a viable economic enterprise, it has overcome many of its initial problems, improved membership participation and control, acquired a working relationship with federal and state agencies as well as established Mississippi coops, and therefore improved its prospects considerably after a very poor start.

The Mileston Farmers Cooperative, located in Lexington (Holmes County), Mississippi, is the oldest of all of the organizations affiliated with the SCDP and the FSC. It was organized in 1941 by the Farm Security Administration and by 1944 was a relatively strong enterprise with 120 members, a cotton gin, five houses, a cooperative grocery store, a blacksmith shop, and seventeen acres of land. Initially, the coop's activities were directed by a manager and bookkeeper provided by FSA. However, after the FSA loan was repaid, these officials were replaced with a management staff selected by the coop's members. Subsequently, due to inefficient and corrupt administration, the grocery store went bankrupt and was leased to a local businessman, the cotton gin became indebted to a local white seed merchant who assumed control of it, and membership declined to thirty-two persons. The coop's board closed the membership, and the organization assumed the character of a private business controlled by a five-man clique.

Through the efforts of SCDP organizer Howard Bailey (a member of the county board of elections, former chairman of the Mississippi Freedom Democratic Party, president of Mississippi Action for Community Education, and a member of the board of the FSC), this coop was revived, and membership increased by more than two hundred between 1967 and 1969. The coop's charter was amended to make all farmers in the area eligible for membership; admission fees were reduced from $300 to $1.00; and a new board of directors, elected in April 1968, made arrangements to liquidate the $33,806 debt owed to the white seed merchant. In 1968, Mileston ginned 751 bales of cotton but ended the season with a $4,000 operating loss. However, with a $5,000 loan from the SCDP, the coop renovated its cotton gin and handled nearly two thousand bales in 1969, thereby reducing its operating deficit. In addition, for the first time, some of the coop's members grew vegetables (a total of 150,000 pounds), which were marketed through the West Batesville Farmers Cooperative. The farmers who participated in this experiment averaged between $250 and $300 each. Mileston also distributed over three hundred tons of fertilizer in 1969.

In the summer of 1969 Mileston initiated a program to help poor farmers and farm workers become beef cattle producers. This project, financed with a grant of $265,153 from OEO and a $100,-000 grant from the Ford Foundation, initially involved eighty trainees, each of whom was to apply for individual FHA loans to be used to purchase equipment, breeding stock, and/or land. Federal and state officials of the FHA cooperated in the development of this project and assured the coop that loans and technical assistance would be provided to the trainees. However, applicants rejected by FHA are eligible for loans from a special $140,000 emergency loan fund.

Each intern in this project will receive on-the-job and classroom instruction in beef production techniques, purchasing and marketing, farm management, and pasture development and maintenance for a three-year period. The training will be provided in three separate phases: Tuskegee Institute in Alabama will provide a special workshop for trainees, centered around techniques of artificial insemination, and will provide each trainee with semen from prize cattle. Additional training will be provided at beef cattle ranches in Illinois. Wilson King, an Illinois beef cattle producer who served as a member of President Johnson's Commission on Rural Poverty, was one of the instigators of the project and is coordinating the training on Illinois farms. King was also chairman of the Illinois FHA State Committee. The Illinois Angus and Hereford Association also has promised to support the project.

In the final phase, training will take place on the farms of the trainees. A special four-man staff coordinates the technical assistance services. Each trainee was to receive a $1,000 stipend ($50 per week) and agreed to train at least one other low-income farmer upon completing the program. Each "graduate" was expected to earn at least $5,000 per year from his beef herd operations.

It was planned for the Mileston Coop to provide a variety of services for the beef cattle project, including the purchasing of seed, feed, fertilizer, and other supplies. The coop also planned to develop a credit union and to handle petroleum products during 1970.

Land Purchasing Associations

The most important requirement for viable agricultural enterprises is the ownership of sufficient land. For a variety of reasons, it has been very difficult for black farmers to acquire and retain land in the rural South. The root of this problem can be traced back to the failure to institute a genuine land reform program when slavery was abolished. However, the most important immediate barriers to black land ownership include inadequate capital and credit resources, racial discrimination in the sale of land, excessive mortgage credit costs, and out-migration. Poor farmers have very limited savings, and it is virtually impossible for them to obtain loans from the white-controlled credit structures in the South which have a long history of discrimination against black people. The record of the federal agencies that were established to help small farmers has been only slightly better. Moreover, in many areas of the South, black people who somehow manage to obtain the necessary financial resources cannot purchase land, especially good land, simply because white landowners refuse to sell to them. According to Calvin Beale, an official in the U.S. Department of Agriculture, auctions in the tobacco country of North Carolina, by no means the state in which black people were most disadvantaged, opened with the declaration that bids would be received from whites only.[2] In general, blacks have been permitted to purchase only small amounts of the very worst land.

Many blacks who own land in the South are finding it difficult to retain it. Because the incomes of these farmers are low, the temptation to mortgage or sell their land is great. "Debt slavery" is therefore widespread, and some black landowners have lost their land through foreclosure. Many of the farms owned by blacks in the South are too small to be economically viable, and limited land resources have hampered their ability to diversify into expanding sectors of southern agriculture (livestock, dairy, poultry, grain, timber) which require larger acreages. Moreover, much of the land owned by blacks in the South is idle or under-utilized. For example, although black farmers owned 4.7 million acres of land in 1964, 2 million acres of this belonged to elderly and part-time, noncommercial farmers who cultivated only half of their crop land.[3]

A number of plans are being considered for the purchase and use of land by poor people in the rural South. One proposal by New Communities, Inc., is that a land trust be set up similar to the Jewish National Fund or several such ventures in the United States. The land trust would buy land and lease it to cooperatives, individuals, or private enterprises. The trust could provide technical assistance, education, training, and management and marketing

[2] Beale, "The Negro in American Agriculture" in *The Amercian Negro Reference Book*, p. 196.
[3] *Ibid.*, p. 201.

skills. The International Independence Institute, Inc., an advocate of this arrangement, believes that the land trust should maintain the land for use by those who work it rather than for land speculators. They see a particular danger that the low-income farmer would lose the land if he had title to it because of the temptation to mortgage it when emergency funds are needed. In early 1970, New Communities, Inc., purchased a 4,800-acre farm and a 900-acre trust of land in Lee County, Georgia, near Albany, which will be settled on a lease basis.

Opponents of the land trust feel that the idea is not likely to be very attractive to poor people in the rural South because of their commitment to private ownership. Moreover, according to this view, individually owned farms are likely to be more efficient if the farmers can receive the necessary training and assistance. Critics of the land trust also feel that land purchase programs would make it possible to turn money over faster, because some individuals could qualify for loans from other sources, like FHA, and return the money which might then be used to buy additional land. Finally, some cooperative leaders resent the implication that poor people cannot manage their own affairs in such a way as to retain control of the land.

There were several other collective land purchases in the South during the 1960s. In 1966 the Delta Opportunities Corporation purchased four hundred acres of land at Wayside, near Greenville, Mississippi, to hold in trust for the Poor People's Conference, a self-help organization inspired by the Delta Ministry, a civil rights affiliate of the National Council of Churches. This farm was purchased for $160,000, $71,000 of which was given by an unidentified donor. Ninety-four blacks who had been displaced from plantations in the area were settled on this property. The FSC and the SCDP also assisted the following land acquisitions in Mississippi: the North Bolivar County Farmers Cooperative, which acquired several hundred acres near Mound Bayou; the Freedom Farm Cooperative, which bought forty acres in Sunflower County; the Mississippi Fish Equity, Inc., which obtained eighty acres in West

Point; and a community group in Monticello, which acquired land used for a coop day care center.

There were at least two land purchase programs in Alabama. The first was in Dallas County in the fall of 1967, when an SCDP organizer, Albert Turner, arranged for twelve evicted families to buy three hundred acres for $45,000, $40,000 of which was borrowed from the FHA and $5,000 from the SCDP. These twelve families marketed vegetables through SWAFCA. A larger organization, the Panola Land Buyers Association, purchased 1,200 acres in Sumpter County, Alabama, to settle sixty-five families evicted from a plantation after a NAACP suit charged the owner with mishandling government checks mailed to tenants on his farms. The SCDP and the Federation provided funds for the option on this property and raised the additional $145,000 for the final purchase from foundations, insurance companies, and individual investors or donors—including a Boston millionaire who agreed to let his contribution become a grant if Panola became a nonprofit corporation and a twenty-year noninterest loan if it became a profit-making corporation. Because the final purchase was delayed by litigation involving a dispute between the former owner of the land and some temporary occupants, other land was leased for the families to farm until the dispute was settled.

CREDIT UNIONS

Sixteen credit unions with a total of about six thousand members and assets of over $350,000 were affiliated with the SCDP and the Federation (see table 3) in the summer of 1969. These organizations were formed to provide a source of loans or to eliminate exploitation by loan sharks, plantation owners, merchants, and other money lenders.

The Greenala Citizens Federal Credit Union, in Greensboro (Hale County), Alabama, was organized in 1961 by a group of civil rights activists under the leadership of Lewis Black, who at that time was a field representative of the Alabama Human Relations Council. Black and his associates formed this organization

Table 3. Credit Unions Affiliated with the Federation of Southern Cooperatives, August 1969

Name	Location	Members	(1969) Assets
Greenala Citizens Federal Credit Union	Greensboro, Ala.	933	$ 65,985
East Alabama Federal Credit Union	Auburn, Ala.	300	7,669
Maryala Citizens Federal Credit Union	Marion, Ala.	115	15,969
Demopolis Citizens Federal Credit Union	Demopolis, Ala.	136	3,869
York Citizens Federal Credit Union	York, Ala.	200	8,000
Unified Singers Federal Credit Union	Thomasville, Ga.	190	6,642
Vermillion Parish Federal Credit Union	Abbeville, La.	300	24,000
St. Pauls Federal Credit Union	Lafayette, La.	700	10,500
Delta Valley Federal Credit Union	Tolula, La.	203	6,260
St. Jules Federal Credit Union	Franklin, La.	630	22,392
College Station Federal Credit Union	Little Rock, Ark.	150	1,900
Shelton Blair Federal Credit Union	Blair, S.C.	100	500
NJEA Federal Credit Union	Marianna, Fla.	101	6,000
Sea Island Federal Credit Union	Beauford, S.C.	300	10,000
St. Francis Federal Credit Union	Greenwood, Miss.	500+	100,800
SEASHA Federal Credit Union	Tuskegee, Ala.	1,100	10,000

SOURCE: Federation of Southern Cooperatives and the Southern Cooperative Development Program.

after local banks and white creditors began to cancel loans to black civil rights participants.

This credit union started with only $42.50 and began making $5.00 loans to needy farmers. Five years later, its membership had grown to 1,300; its assets had increased to $67,000; and it had made several loans to help its member purchase farm supplies, medical services, food, clothing, and other items. Eleven of these loans enabled small landowners to save their land from foreclosures.

Greenala suffered a setback in 1967 when delinquencies reduced its cash reserves below the amount required to maintain a federal charter. Within two months, however, the coop strengthened its collection procedures and met the federal auditors' requirements.

The next year, Greenala lost several of its members and $30,000 of its assets because federal examiners ruled that some members of organizations (churches, other coops, and civil rights groups) which had invested in Greenala lived outside the credit union's assigned territory. Despite these difficulties, however, Greenala has continued to expand its membership and assets. The chart below summarizes the financial statements of Greenala from October 3, 1967, through July 31, 1969.

	October 31, 1967	June 30, 1968	July 31, 1969
Membership	850	920	933
Total assets	$72,489.59	$62,624.94	$65,984.54
Total loans	52,555.18	36,240.86	20,364.10
Shares	68,524.25	58,084.45	58,084.45
Delinquencies	52	20	20

SOURCE: Southern Cooperative Development Program Reports.

FISHING COOPERATIVES

Our sample includes a number of low-income fishing cooperatives, the largest of which is the Florida Fisherman's Association (FFA), organized at Ruskin, Florida, in 1967. FFA provided processing and marketing for its eighty-eight members.

FFA's main instigator was a local fish dealer who encouraged his suppliers to establish a cooperative after his own private business ran into financial difficulties. There were seventy-four fishermen in the original founding group, 88 percent of whom had incomes below $3,000. With a $245,000 economic opportunity loan from the FHA, FFA purchased the fish dealer's processing plant and other facilities. The dealer was retained as manager when the coop began operations in October 1967, partly because the FHA insisted on it, and received a 5 percent commission on sales of members' fish and 1 percent on nonmembers' sales rather than a fixed salary. FFA grossed over $243,800 its first season, and its sales exceeded $380,000 the following year.

Because of the coop, FFA members purchased supplies at lower prices and have received high prices for their fish. Fifteen members who earned less than $3,000 a year when they joined the coop earned over $4,500 in 1968. The coop also provided employment for an additional seventy-five men who work on the members' boats and share a percentage of the catch.

As the above data indicated, FFA is a relatively successful enterprise, and much of its success can be attributed to the administrative and marketing effectiveness of the manager. The coop also has received technical assistance from FHA and the Fish and Wildlife Commission.

Membership support is strong. Each of the members has purchased a $100 share, and most are active in the affairs of the coop. Although most of the members are white, 20 percent are Indians and Mexican Americans.

The coop was making plans to develop a credit union, a boatbuilding coop, and a program to train captains to man the fishing vessels in the summer of 1969 and had applied to FHA and OEO for additional funds.

The Mississippi Fish Equity was established in West Point (Clay County), Mississippi, by low-income farmers who wanted to supplement their cotton earnings by raising channel catfish in ponds on their farms. They were assisted by officials at nearby Mary Holmes Junior College, who sponsored a feasibility study showing that catfish farming could become an important new income source for small farmers.

The coop had only twenty-five members in June 1969, less than half of whom already had ponds, but it had plans to include two or three hundred farmers in eight counties in east central Mississippi. MFE received a $160,000 loan from the Presbyterian Church in 1969 to be used for operating capital, processing facilities, equipment, and land. The SCDP granted MFE $500 and assigned it a full-time field organizer.

The Hilton Head Fishing Cooperative (HHFC), on Hilton Head Island in Beaufort County, South Carolina, was formed in January 1967 by ten low-income fishermen to process and market shrimp, purchase supplies, and use docking and marine railway services cooperatively. HHFC's immediate objective was to improve the productivity and incomes of its members; however, its long-range goal was to establish a large-scale, seafood enterprise that would be owned and operated by the poor black community of Hilton Head.

The original promoter of the coop was Freddie Chisolm, a fifty-six-year-old fisherman who was the first black man on the island to build or own a commercial fishing vessel. Prior to the formation of the coop, most of the black fishermen in the area worked as "sharecatchers" for absentee white boat owners, because it was virtually impossible for a black fisherman to obtain a loan with which to purchase a boat. According to Chisolm, this had been the main barrier to previous attempts to form a coop.

This situation changed in 1964 when the FHA economic opportunity loan program was established. Most of HHFC's members purchased their vessels with loans from this source. However, one member obtained a loan from SBA and another from a local commercial bank.

Most of the coop's initial capital requirements were met in June

1968 with a $66,290 FHA loan used to purchase a dock, a processing plant, and equipment. However, the FHA loan did not provide funds for operating machinery or for a freezing plant, despite the fact that these items were recommended in a feasibility study sponsored by OEO. In addition, the FHA required that most of the construction work be contracted out for $15,000, even though the feasibility study suggested that the members do most of the construction.

HHFC began its operations on October 1, 1968, when the construction of its processing plant was completed, but because of inadequate facilities and low volume, revenue did not cover costs, and the coop ended the season with a $2,104.23 loss.

HHFC does not appear to have any serious management problems. The manager established a good working relationship with the board of directors and was thoroughly familiar with shrimp processing and packing operations but needed additional training in bookkeeping, sales promotion, and personnel supervision, much of which is being provided by FSC.

The membership of the coop in 1970 was active and closely knit and exercised effective membership control. Indeed, the only member not on the board of directors was the manager, and membership patronage was very strong. During the coop's first year, members invested $7,285.80, including $2,500 in the form of "sweat equity." The investments, while less than the ideal of 20 percent of initial capital requirements, were substantial and significantly higher than for most low-income southern coops.

The main problem with the membership is that it is too small. Apparently, some board members are opposed to enlargement for fear new members might be disruptive. However, the major barrier to membership expansion seems to be that few of the twenty nonmember black fishermen in the area own vessels—a requirement for membership in HHFC. Most of the potential members of the coop are sharecatchers who operate vessels owned by whites. HHFC has a practical as well as a moral responsibility to encourage and assist these men in obtaining loans from FHA and other sources so they can purchase vessels and become eligible for coop membership.

In order to prosper, HHFC must increase its volume, but this will require a larger membership. It is possible that HHFC could increase its volume by attracting more patronage from nonmembers, but if this happens, the organization runs the risk of losing its status as a coop, which must obtain over half of its income from members.

In 1969 HHFC received grants of $20,000 from the Episcopal Church and $29,000 from the Ford Foundation to extend its docks to accommodate more and larger vessels, acquire additional machinery to make it possible to process more shrimp in less time at lower costs, expand its physical plant to provide more freezing and storage space so that shrimp can be retained for better off-season prices, hire additional staff, and establish an emergency loan fund. These acquisitions enabled the coop to increase volume and nonmember patronage, making it possible for HHFC to compete with other local shrimp processors.

Although some of the coop's members clear as much as $5,000 a season from shrimp fishing, it does not provide employment for very many people, and most of its members work elsewhere during off seasons.

In order to expand, HHFC plans to accumulate more capital by reinvesting annual profits, acquiring other income-producing enterprises, and diversifying into crabs, oysters, and other fish products.

HHFC is lessening the dependence of its members upon white boat owners and has enabled some black fishermen to remain with their families rather than moving to Florida and Mexico with the white-owned boats after the South Carolina shrimping season ends.

HHFC also has established a credit union which will benefit nonmembers as well as members.

The Federation of Southern Cooperatives subsidizes the manager's salary and has assigned a field representative to develop other cooperative projects on the island as well as to help HHFC.

CONSUMER COOPERATIVES

Several cooperative grocery stores are owned and operated by poor people. Probably the most successful of these is the Greenwood Cooperative Club (GCC) in Greenwood, Mississippi. GCC was begun in 1964 by Father Nathaniel Machesky, a white Franciscan priest, as an outgrowth of the St. Francis Federal Credit Union, from which it obtained much of its initial capital resources. GCC also received a $35,000 loan for seed capital from the Franciscan religious order. This coop began as a small buying club in the basement of St. Frances Catholic Church but subsequently expanded into a retail marketing enterprise with over eight hundred members. After more than $11,000 in shares was sold, GCC was incorporated in 1965 and purchased a small grocery store in February 1967. In November of the following year, the coop leased a larger supermarket, which is its present location.

GCC provides its members with groceries at substantial savings, has made profits every year, and has paid an average of 3 percent a year in dividends and an average of 2 percent in patronage refunds. Financial data for 1967 through July 1969 are summarized below.

	1967	1968	January–July 1969
Gross sales	$99,004.02	$178,363.30	$176,421.51
Net profit	2,966.84	4,969.31	—
Average daily sales	370.80	577.22	980.11
Dividends	2%	5%	—
Patronage refunds	3%	2%	—

SOURCE: SCDP Reports.

GCC's sales volume has increased each year, was averaging more than $30,000 per month in the summer of 1970, and was expected to reach an annual rate of $300,000 by the end of that year.

Much of GCC's success can be attributed to efficient and dedicated management and staff. Much of the initial work at the store was done by unpaid volunteers. The close relationship between the GCC and the St. Francis Credit Union has also had a positive influence, because the credit union has made it possible for many low-income families in Greenwood to break their dependence upon neighborhood stores to which they were indebted.

GCC also received strong support from the local black community when the store and Father Machesky were opposed by whites. The coop also has benefited from a black boycott against local white merchants that had been in effect for over a year in the summer of 1970 when GCC was planning a membership drive to enroll at least seven thousand from among twenty thousand potential members in the area.

The SCDP loaned this coop $4,400 to renovate and enlarge the supermarket and provided funds for management trainee salaries.

The Cash and Carry Grocery (C&C), in Greensboro, Alabama, was established in 1966 by forty-five blacks who felt white-owned stores were charging excessive prices for inferior merchandise. Capital was raised through $5.00 membership shares and a loan from the Greenala Credit Union. During its first year of operation, C&C's gross sales were $50,000, and the coop barely broke even, but sales increased and a small profit was earned the following year. The main problems confronting this coop were small volume, inadequate support by the black community, and stiff competition from white-owned neighborhood stores which offer credit.

The SCDP and the Federation have helped C&C by providing loans to expand its inventory. In addition, SCDP and Federation field representatives have organized buying clubs which purchase through C&C.

The Mid-South Oil Consumers Cooperative (MSOCC), located in Whiteville, Tennessee, operates a service station and distributes gasoline, oil, tires, batteries, and other automotive products and services to its 350 members and about 250 nonmember patrons in a three-county (Fayette, Hardeman, Haywood) area.

This organization, formed in 1965, grew out of the voter registration drives of the early 1960s. When MSOCC was established, most blacks in the three-county area could not obtain petroleum products because local white distributors refused to sell to blacks who had registered to vote. For almost a year, therefore, these people had to drive several miles to Memphis and northern Mississippi for supplies.

This experience caused a small group of black farmers, led by E. R. Shockley, a retired black county extension agent, to establish their own petroleum business. They began as a small buying club and raised $4,700 by selling preferred stock and $100 membership fees. In the fall of 1965 MSOCC obtained a charter and secured a $49,000 loan from FHA for a building, bulk storage facilities, tanks, pumps, and two trucks to bring gasoline from the Missouri Farmers Cooperative in Memphis to its members at a savings of about 5 cents per gallon.

During its first three years of operation, Mid-South's annual net profit averaged between $5,000 and $6,000 and gross sales were about $80,000 a year.

Although Mid-South seems to have done well at first, it later encountered financial difficulties for a number of reasons, including the seasonal demand for petroleum products in rural Tennessee; improper inventory control, which caused the coop to fail to maintain proper margins between costs and prices; poor utilization of labor, which caused manpower costs to be too high for the coop's operating volume; and credit policies that caused excessive delinquencies. Mid-South developed these problems after its first manager, who apparently had been responsible for the organization's initial stability, became ill and died. Father McKnight and the SCDP did much to correct some of Mid-South's problems and therefore probably played a vital role in helping the cooperative to survive.

HANDICRAFT COOPERATIVES

Ten handicraft cooperatives with about 1,160 members, summarized in table 4, are affiliated with the Federation. Most of these organizations provide supplementary sources of income to farmers' wives. Five of these coops in Appalachia were all white, one

Table 4. Handicraft Cooperatives Affiliated with the Federation of Southern Cooperatives, August 1969

Name and Location	Members	Products
Basic Enterprises,* Hyti, Mo.	46	Dolls, aprons, potholders, stuffed animals
Blueridge Hearthside Crafts Association,* Sugar Grove, N.C.	51	Dolls, cornhusk items, wood carvings
Floristas Del Rio Grande,** Laredo, Tex.	50	Artificial flowers, jewelry
Grassroots Craftsmen of the Appalachian Mountains,* Breathitt and Wolf Counties, Ky.	40	Dolls, hats, brooms, toys
Freedom Quilting Bee,*** Gee's Bend, Ala.	96	Quilts, aprons, dresses, African dashikis
Laurel Forks Crafts,* Frakes, Ky.	12	Dolls, cornhusk items, jewelry
Mountain Community Crafts* Wilder, Tenn.	25	Split pine benches, fireside bellows, note clips, dolls
Wyoming County Originals,* Beckley, W. Va.	30	Ponchos, pajamas, pillows, skirts, dresses, quilted items
Poor Peoples Corporation,*** Jackson, Miss.	800	Candles, pocketbooks, dolls, wood carvings, belts
Freedom Craft Candy Coop,*** Edwards, Miss.	10	Pecan and peanut candies

SOURCE: Federation of Southern Cooperatives.
  * Membership all white.
 ** Membership Mexican American.
*** Membership Negro.

was composed of Mexican Americans, and the remainder were all black.

The most celebrated of these handicraft cooperatives were the Freedom Quilting Bee (FQB) and the Poor People's Corporation (PPC), although some of those in Appalachia, with a longer handicraft tradition, are economically more successful.

The Poor People's Corporation (PPC), organized in Jackson, Mississippi, in 1965, had established thirteen producers' cooperatives and Liberty House, a marketing coop, with sales outlets in Jackson; Cambridge, Massachusetts; Yellow Springs, Ohio; Madison, Wisconsin; San Francisco; and Detroit by 1969. PPC also operated a publishing company, a film-making organization, a training center, and a revolving loan fund in Jackson, and provided marketing, training, and technical assistance to its affiliates. PPC's organizer and executive director is Jesse Morris, a former SNCC field worker with a degree in economics from the University of California at Los Angeles.

Each of PPC's coops is a separate business organization controlled by the workers who elect managers and make other policy decisions. Each member coop is required to sell through Liberty House, which, in addition to its retail outlets, operates a mail order catalog system. Nine of PPC's coops produce sewn crafts, two produce leather crafts, one produces wood crafts, and one produces candles. In 1968 the corporation provided employment for over two hundred former sharecroppers.

Liberty House is owned by the member cooperatives and is controlled by a board of directors made up of representatives from each. In addition to its marketing functions, Liberty House sets policies on a wide variety of matters for the coops and their members. For example, it operates a group health program for all workers, purchases glasses for all workers who need them, and requires that each coop member be a registered voter.

Although it has received some outside support, PPC is almost unique among the new poor people's cooperatives in having been financed mainly by the poor people themselves. Funds from government agencies have not been available because the corporation's program was deemed to be unworkable,[4] and "access to large capital grants from OEO or loans from FHA were also denied because of powerful local and national interests."[5] The organization, therefore, has been forced to proceed slowly with its economic activities.

Although it has no well-formulated plan or ideology, PPC seems to be more opposed to working with the white establishment and

[4] Ben Poage, "A Look at Southern Co-ops," *Appalachian Outlook*, January 1969, p. 19.
[5] *Ibid.*

71

is more suspicious of government programs than most of the other predominantly black cooperatives. PPC's leaders have opposed guaranteed annual income plans as "another extension of a bankrupt welfare plan. Like the present welfare system, it will be used to shut up the poor rather than to participate in mainstream American decisions."[6]

PPC has produced only modest economic results for most of its participants, who rarely earn as much as $1.25 an hour. Earnings were reported to have ranged from $15.00 to $50.00 a week in 1968, and they have averaged $20.00 to $25.00 a week.[7] Despite these low earnings, prices seem relatively high for products that depend largely on a sympathetic market.

But these accomplishments are not inconsequential in view of the obstacles confronting PPC. The SNCC field workers who launched the organization had little or no business experience, and handicraft production, a marginal activity under the best circumstances, had to be learned by the former sharecroppers.

In spite of these difficulties, the absence of massive outside assistance, and the marginal economic nature of PPC's activities, PPC has apparently instilled considerable loyalty among its membership. In many ways PPC will test the ability of a group of very poor black people, with only limited outside assistance, to make a viable economic enterprise out of handicraft production.

Although the Federation made a $5,000 emergency loan to PPC in 1968, there has been little communication or cooperation between the two groups since then.

The Freedom Quilting Bee (FQB), at Gee's Bend, Alabama, an all-black rural community in Wilcox County, had ninety-six members in 1969. FQB was organized in March 1965 by a group of poor black women to produce and market quilts and other items of stitchery in a desperate attempt to develop a new source of income after the mechanization of cotton farming and reprisals for

[6] *Ibid.*

[7] *Ibid.* and *New York Times,* July 21, 1968, which reported a range of $15.00 to $30.00 a week.

civil rights activities caused almost total unemployment in the area. The Reverend Francis X. Walter, a young white Episcopal priest, played a major role in the FQB's organization.

Quilting, an established art in Gee's Bend, is the only genuine skill, other than farming, possessed by the residents of this destitute community. When the coop was formed, the average annual income of its members was less than $800.

The FQB was formally incorporated in 1965, and its initial capital, a $350 grant from the Southern Regional Council, was used to cover organizing expenses and materials. A $5,000 grant from the New York Foundation enabled the coop to hire two managers. Additional funds were raised from members—each of whom donates one quilt a year as dues—and through cash donations from outside sympathizers solicited by the Alabama Human Relations Council.

During its first two years of operation the FQB marketed most of its quilts (which were sewn in the members' homes from cheap scrap material bought wholesale from clothing manufacturing plants) locally, and members earned an average of less than 20 cents per hour. Total sales for 1965–1966 were less than $6,000 while total sales for 1966–1967 were only $9,100.

The SCDP's assistance enabled FQB to make steady progress from 1967 to 1969. In January 1968, for example, the SCDP employed two handicraft specialists (Stanley Sellengut and his assistant, Sara Stine) to help with product design, marketing, and management. As a result of changes initiated by Sellengut (substitution of high quality materials for scrap materials, doubling of prices, new machinery, increased productivity, creation and standardization of new designs, and marketing through large retail stores and handicraft outlets throughout the country), the coop's sales volume more than doubled during 1968 and the first half of 1969, and the members' hourly earnings increased to about 65 cents. While this is somewhat less than Sellengut's goal of one dollar per hour in one year, six members made $1,000 or more in 1968.

The SCDP also made FQB a $5,000 loan to purchase new materials and a truck and to meet general operating expenses. Two SCDP grants totaling $4,000 were used to pay the manager's salary in 1968 and 1969. In addition, the SCDP assigned a full-time field organizer to help FQB with day-to-day problems and to provide cooperative education. The SCDP has also held training sessions for the coop's board of directors. In 1969 the FQB built a new $20,000 sewing center for which the Federation provided a $9,000 loan. The National Council of Negro Women also provided $10,000, which the coop used to purchase twenty-three acres of land.

Garment Cooperatives

The most controversial of the new low-income cooperatives in the South are those which produce and market garments. These organizations typically subcontract with larger clothing manufacturers in urban areas to sew a certain amount of clothing within a specified period of time at a set price. Cloth (usually pre-cut), trimmings, and packaging materials are provided by the manufacturer in return for the labor, thread, machinery, and plant, which are provided by the coop. In some instances, both parties share shipping costs, and the supplier or middleman sells or leases the machines to the coop.

Two "cut and sew" coops have affiliated with the Federation. Appalachian Enterprises, in Mineral Bluff, Georgia, was established in 1967 by ten poor white women after an unsuccessful 365-day strike against the Levi Strauss Company at Blue Ridge, Georgia. The strikers rejected a contract negotiated with the assistance of an AFL-CIO representative and decided to establish a cooperative garment factory. These white women obtained a $4,000 grant from the SCLC, rented two rooms in the back of a wholesale company warehouse, subcontracted with a clothing manufacturer in Atlanta, and began operations. All of the members, from the janitor to the manager, accepted the same rate of pay, and each of the members was on the board of directors, which determined all management policies.

Unfortunately, this first contract was a serious failure. The coop's members were overworked and underpaid, producing clothing for the Atlanta company which purchased the coop's products at substandard prices. These losses and its inability to obtain new contracts caused a two-month shutdown in February 1968.

As a result of its problems, the coop was dissolved and reorganized as a private corporation (Mineral Bluffs, Inc.) after the organization was given $12,000 by a private benefactor and technical and business advice from an Atlanta businessman. The twelve "owners" continued to work for the same wages as the "employees," but they each earned less than the minimum wage.

The Federation helped the Mineral Bluffs group by hiring a certified public accountant to set up an accounting system and to train one of the members in bookkeeping, providing a $3,651.20 loan to pay the salaries of the employees until payments were received from a contract which had not yet been completed. The Federation continued to assist the organization after it changed from a cooperative to a private corporation and even made a $250 grant to help them get incorporated. The Federation also made a $2,-382.70 loan to the organization in February 1969, which it used to make up back pay for unemployment compensation, because the U.S. Department of Labor had threatened to close down the plant.

Another cut and sew enterprise, the Green-Hale Sewing Cooperative, was formed in Greensboro, Alabama, in 1967 by several unemployed low-income women from Green and Hale Counties. None of these women had ever held full-time jobs, although some had worked as domestics for $5.00 to $10.00 per week. They felt that sewing would be an easy craft for them to learn.

They enlisted the support of Randolph Blackwell (a close aide of the late Dr. Martin Luther King), director of the Southern Rural Advancement Project sponsored by the Citizens' Crusade against Poverty, and Lewis Black, field representative of the

Alabama Council on Human Relations. The women raised $43 among themselves and, with the assistance of Black and Blackwell, obtained a $500 grant from the Southern Regional Council and a $200 grant from the Rural Advancement Project. Black also helped the group obtain funds from the Greenala Citizens Federal Credit Union and secure a $2,000 loan from a commercial bank in nearby Moundville, Alabama.

The group then negotiated a contract with an Atlanta-based garment broker and consultant, who agreed to provide a four-week training program, the machines (the coop had the option to buy or lease the machines for one year), and subcontract work for $2,400 per week during the six-month period following the completion of the training period. The coop agreed to provide space and facilities for the training program.

Unfortunately, financial losses resulting from having to rework the first order without pay and the consultant's failure to pay the coop caused serious financial problems for Green-Hale. The coop was therefore unable to meet its payroll, purchase supplies, or cover its operating expenses.

In 1969 Lewis Black arranged a contract between Green-Hale and the L. V. Myles Clothing Company in New York, which sent an experienced company representative to manage the coop and to supervise training. As a result, production increased within a relatively short period of time, and the women were earning an average of $35.00 per week. In 1970 the coop's manager was confident that production would continue to improve, making it possible for the women to earn the minimum wage.

COMMUNITY DEVELOPMENT ORGANIZATIONS

There are two multipurpose, low-income cooperatives which do not fit neatly into any of the above categories and which, therefore, might be called community development cooperatives. Because they are "umbrella" organizations which meet a variety of needs, these community cooperatives could have great significance for rural development.

The Southern Consumer Cooperative (SCC) had 2,082 members in twenty chapters in southwestern Louisiana in the summer of 1969. SCC was organized at Lafayette in 1961 by Father McKnight and his associates and incorporated in 1964. SCC is primarily an investment cooperative with the following subsidiary operations: a loan company known as Peoples Enterprise; the Acadian Delight Bakery; the Southern Consumers Education Foundation; several grocery and fertilizer buying clubs; and a Blue Cross medical health insurance plan. SCC's assets increased to more than $200,000 in 1969 from less than $25,000 in 1964. Each member pays $5.00 into the educational fund and pledges to invest an additional $300, usually at the rate of $1.00 a month. These funds become capital for the bakery and the loan company. By 1969 more than $162,000 had been invested by members.

The Acadian Delight Bakery was established by SCC at Lake Charles, Louisiana, in 1964. Much of Acadian Delight's initial capital was from a $35,000 Small Business Administration economic opportunity loan used to purchase a plant and equipment. The bakery operated at a loss for its first three years, primarily because of marketing and management difficulties.

The bakery earned a small profit ($1,600) for the first time in 1967–1968 due to a large national contract for 25,000 fruitcakes with the Barracini Candy Company in New York. The Barracini Company increased its purchases in 1969, and twenty-six food brokers throughout the nation agreed to handle the bakery's products.

The bakery employs a regular work force of twenty-seven people, half of whom are trainees whose wages are partially subsidized by a $10,000 MDTA grant. During the peak season, the work force increases to thirty or forty.

The main problems facing the bakery are the low productivity of its labor force, cost accounting problems, internal friction, and losses caused by the embezzlement of thousands of dollars by a white manager who had not been located by the spring of 1970.

The SCDP has helped Acadian Delight by providing loans of $20,000 for emergency operating capital and supplies; providing $4,000 during 1968 and 1969 in management subsidy grants; hiring special consultants to help the bakery with its sales during 1967–1968; and assigning field organizers to help increase sales to SCC members. As with many other marginal enterprises, however, Acadian Delight's future appeared uncertain in the summer of 1970 because its fortunes are volatile, depending heavily on decisions and actions by relatively few people.

The Southern Consumers Education Foundation (SCEF) is a separately chartered nonprofit organization to undertake general as well as cooperative education. It was established in 1964 and is financed by SCC membership initiation fees and grants from government and private sources. SCEF sponsored several projects, including the OEO-financed Sweet Potato Alert Program in 1965, which led to the formation of the Grand Marie Vegetable Producers Cooperative; a Head Start program for more than two thousand poor preschool children in eight southwest Louisiana parishes; and an OEO-sponsored management training program for the Vermillion Parish Federal Credit Union. The SCEF's largest and most important project, however, was the Southern Cooperative Development Program (SCDP).

Like SWAFCA, Southern Consumers is situated in an extremely hostile environment and has suffered because of harassment from local politicians and other racists who accused the coop of being a communist organization. SCC's records were seized in a raid by the local sheriff and district attorney in April 1967, and it was investigated by the Louisiana Un-American Activity Committee. SCC obtained a temporary restraining order from the Fifth Circuit Court of Appeals, and, after a lengthy hearing, a federal district court ordered the return of the coop's books and a cessation of harassment by the district attorney. However, as was probably their intention, these attacks shook the confidence of SCC's members in the organization and caused several of them to withdraw their investments and discontinue patronizing it.

The South East Alabama Self-Help Association (SEASHA), based in Tuskegee, is a multipurpose cooperative serving the rural poor in twelve counties (Barbour, Bullock, Coosa, Crenshaw, Elmore, Lee, Lowndes, Macon, Montgomery, Pike, Russell, and Tallapoosa, one of which (Lowndes) overlaps with SWAFCA. SEASHA grew out of a series of Tuskegee Institute Community outreach programs. Its origins can be traced back to 1963 when a group of sixty students, under the leadership of P. B. Phillips (Dean of Students at Tuskegee), formed the Community Action Corps (CAC) to help low-income people in the area.

In 1965 CAC established the Tuskegee Institute Summer Education Project (TISEP) with a federal grant to provide tutorial and cultural enrichment to over eight thousand students and adults in southeast Alabama.

In 1967 TISEP grew into the Tuskegee Institute Community Education Program (TICEP) with grants from the U.S. Office of Education and the Office of Economic Opportunity. This program, involving more than 1,850 different students, provided a wide range of educational and welfare services to rural poor people in twelve predominantly rural Alabama counties. TICEP's staff comprised indigenous leaders, students and graduates, and professionally trained social workers and provided over 50,000 people with such services as preventing home evictions and school dropouts, paving streets, extending public utilities to low-income communities, securing medical and legal services, and providing food, clothing, transportation, day care centers, and recreational facilities.

It became increasingly clear to TICEP's leaders, however, that the problems of poor people in rural Alabama could not be solved through temporary programs affecting only a small fraction of the area's people. Therefore, in May 1967 Dr. Phillips and others organized the South East Alabama Self-Help Association (SEASHA), and it was incorporated as a nonprofit corporation with headquarters in a building long identified with the poor. It was owned by the Farmers Coop of Montgomery County and was used for meetings and rest rooms by poor black farmers and their families in the days when few other such facilities were available to blacks. SEASHA's board of directors was made up of sixty members, five from each of the twelve counties; its executive committee consists of the board of directors and fifteen representatives, one elected from each county and three elected at large. SEASHA's technical staff is made up of a director, a deputy director, a business manager, a credit union coordinator, a livestock project manager, a coordinator for field activities, a veterinarian, a swine specialist, veterinary aides, a bookkeeper, recruiters, community development aides, secretaries, and other clerical assistants.

Because of inadequate finances (membership fees are only 50 cents per year), SEASHA did not become active until October 1968, when it received an OEO grant of $479,536 to establish a twelve-county feeder pig cooperative, a federal credit union, and to undertake feasibility studies of various nonagricultural development projects.

The SEASHA Feeder Pig Management and Marketing Coop (SFPMMC) was established in June 1969 to help poor farmers diversify into livestock production. SFPMMC began with 24 members, 2 from each of the 12 counties, but by March 1969 membership had increased to 250. In May 1970, 32 members had established feeder pig units (ten sows and one boar) with purebred stock provided by the coop. The coop also provided feed, purchased in bulk quantities on a monthly basis, and marketing facilities. Technical assistance and training in production techniques, buying and selling practices, farm management and accounting is provided by a special field staff which consists of six swine specialists (one for two counties), twelve recruiters (two per county), one veterinarian, and two part-time veterinary aides. These farmers also receive operating loans ranging from $1,500 to $2,500 used to purchase equipment and construct boar pens, night sheds, loading chutes, and feed troughs. SEASHA is attempting to transfer these loans to the FHA so that it can revolve its $50,000 loan fund and involve additional farmers. In this way, with a small additional grant from OEO or some private organization, SEASHA hoped to expand to at least ten farmers in each county. Its ability to do this, however, was thwarted by a dispute between OEO and FHA over administration of the opportunity loan program, which caused these funds to be frozen in April 1969.

SFPMMC has held a number of sales since November 1969, when its first group of pigs were marketed, which demonstrated that poor farmers could become successful commercial swine producers with adequate financial and technical assistance.

SEASHA's feeder pig operations clearly give considerable promises for improving the incomes of its members. For example, in August 1969 there were 24 families involved in this activity with 148 members whose family incomes averaged $2,294 (about $372 per family member) and ranged from $700 to $6,720. Six families had incomes above $3,000 a year.

These farmers have average incomes which probably about doubled those of the members of other coops affiliated with the FSC. The average school grade completed was 6.8, which also was probably above the average of other poor people's coop members at that time.

Between October 1969 and May 1970 these twenty-four families sold 2,055 pigs, on which they had net profits of about $333 per family; the range was from $93 to $554. The average income of SEASHA's feeder pig participants thus increased about 15 percent per family over a seven-month period, which represented a significant addition to the incomes of these families even though the project is in its initial stages.

The SEASHA Federal Credit Union (SFCU) was chartered in April 1969 and had 1,700 members by February 1970, who had invested a total of $110,050 at $5.00 per share. The credit union received valuable assistance from the Alabama Credit Union League, of which SEASHA is a member. As of February 1970 three hundred members had received loans which totaled $90,-511.92. Proceeds from interest on loans netted $1,544.38.

In March 1969 SEASHA received a $74,610 grant from the Economic Development Administration for a business and job development program. OEO hired a Washington, D.C., consulting firm to make a series of feasibility studies of possible ventures to be undertaken by SEASHA, and in the summer of 1970 SEASHA was negotiating with a plastics and a textile firm to locate in the area. The plastics plant would employ about sixty workers.

SEASHA also purchased an option of 335 acres in Tuskegee for its new headquarters and an industrial and housing development project for low-income people.

SUMMARY

The agricultural marketing and supply coops are the most numerous of the FSC's low-income affiliates and have the most members. Although none of these organizations could be considered a clear success in the summer of 1970, most had improved their operations, usually with help from the SCDP and the Federation. The main problems confronting the agricultural coops are under-capitalization, inefficient management, marketing difficulties, and insufficient volume caused by inadequate membership participation.

Agricultural coops undoubtedly have improved their members' real incomes by increasing the prices they received, lowering their costs, lessening their dependence on local planters and brokers, making greater diversification possible, promoting more efficient land use, and improving their farming and management practices.

The agricultural coops have also benefited nonmember, low-income farmers in their respective localities by forcing private buyers and other competitors to increase prices paid for produce and to lower prices charged for supplies.

The credit unions probably will have less difficulty surviving than the other low-income coops because they require less capital and management than other types and are based on the fairly universal need for places to save and sources of credit. In the rural South, credit unions also have made it possible for the poor to use their modest financial resources to support cooperative activities. The main problems confronting credit unions are capital shortages, management and record-keeping difficulties, and delinquencies on loan repayments.

Consumer coops also show considerable promise, especially when they deal in widely used items like petroleum products, farm supplies, and groceries and other household goods. Some consumer coops have achieved substantial savings for their members and seem to be most successful in places where they have good managers and where whites refuse to sell to blacks who have engaged in civil rights activities or where blacks are boycotting white-owned stores.

The handicraft and garment coops are very marginal and unstable enterprises which are significant only as sources of supplementary income. The handicraft coops seem to be most successful in areas like Appalachia and Gee's Bend, where there is a strong craft tradition. The main problem confronting the handicraft coops is marketing. Most of these organizations depend upon "sympathetic markets," which are very unreliable and difficult to locate.

The garment coops also suffer from marketing difficulties. Most operate as subcontractors to and almost completely at the mercy of larger clothing firms. The garment industry has a reputation for instability and for being a "cut-throat" industry characterized by "shady deals." Many garment contractors are "fly by night" firms which have moved from the North or urban areas of the South in order to escape unionization. There also is some question of whether or not the coop structure is adaptable to manufacturing enterprises. As Appalachian Enterprises' experience illustrates, collective policy making is likely to be inefficient and complicated because it is difficult to discipline or replace inefficient workers who are also members of boards of directors. Management is likely to be a problem for all coops, but it is especially serious with cooperative manufacturing activities which historically have either failed or been transformed into corporations. At the same time, it is hard to argue against the garment coops, which provide skills to unskilled people and, in the case of Green-Hale, more than triple the incomes of women who are earning as little as $5.00 or $10.00 per week as domestics.

Although they have great difficulty acquiring capital and face many of the other managerial problems confronting the low-income coops in the South, the land purchasing associations are essential to the future of poor farmers. However, small farmers have had great difficulty acquiring and retaining land. Perhaps the experiments currently under way will develop model financial and organizational methods for the acquisition of land which can be supported by public policy.

The fishing coops seem to be doing well in most places, primarily because there is a strong demand for their products. The main problem confronting the HHFCA and FFA is their members' inability to acquire their own vessels. This has made it hard for the coops to expand their membership and thereby increase their volume. The success of the catfish coops will be determined by the extent to which these organizations can obtain land, technical assistance, and machinery, and can do a good job of marketing their fish.

Because of the multiplicity of the problems facing the rural poor, the multipurpose approach of the development coops seems to have considerable promise. Under capable leadership, and supported by an entire community, they can have a greater impact on a wider variety of the obstacles to improving the status of black people in the rural South.

5

Appraisal

Our review of the poor people's cooperatives makes it clear that they are not likely to have a very significant impact unless they either gain considerable strength or stimulate rural reforms to overcome some of the deeply entrenched causes of rural poverty. Really significant changes in the conditions of the rural poor will depend on developments in agricultural policy; economic development; manpower programs; education; health and welfare; and measures to combat racial discrimination in the sale of land, access to credit, and government services to farmers. Cooperatives can do something to stimulate effective policies, but they probably cannot have much impact on the problems of rural poverty unless they produce changes in these areas.

For example, low-income cooperatives have been very fragile organizations mainly because they are made up of small farmers who are having great difficulty maintaining their competitive positions. The displacement of small farmers is due in part to U.S. agricultural policy and in part to technological and economic forces. While many people who are being displaced can and should find better income-producing opportunities in nonagricultural jobs, many others might, with appropriate public policies, be able to earn adequate livings in agriculture or in a combination of agricultural and rural nonagricultural jobs. For example, agricultural reforms which subsidized labor, instead of land and capital, could change the prospects for small farmers and their organizations.

Similarly, passage of the proposed Family Assistance Plan (FAP) could have profound effects on the rural South by doubling and tripling the incomes of many poor families. The FAP probably would strengthen coops by providing an income base upon which poor farmers could build and give them a measure of economic, and hence political, independence. The lower cost of living in rural areas might halt out-migration, particularly for older uneducated farmers. On the other hand, FAP and better rural-urban manpower linkages might accelerate the out-migration of younger, better educated people.

In the absence of these kinds of reforms, however, the prospects for poor farmers and their coops are not very bright. Without public policies supporting them, coops will be able to do little more than fight a delaying action to ease the economic burdens of those who cannot find rural or urban nonagricultural jobs.

On the other hand, it is possible to conceive of circumstances in which the coops could become a voice for many of the rural poor in the South and, joining with urban friends in and out of the South, produce some significant changes in those institutions responsible for rural poverty. Cooperatives, for example, could join with unions, civil rights groups, and interested foundations in providing a voice for small farmers and the rural poor in the formulation of public policy. In the absence of such representation, agricultural and rural development policies will continue to be made by, and reflect the interests of, the most affluent farmers and their political allies.

In order to accomplish their potential, however, coops clearly must become viable economic enterprises. The remainder of this chapter appraises the coops' chances for economic success by comparing their present and probable future performance with success criteria derived from cooperative experience in this country and abroad.

Essential Ingredients

In order to survive and maintain internal cohesion, a coop clearly must meet the needs of members or potential members more effectively than the alternative means available to them.

The establishment of the cooperative also should be based upon careful planning. The organization's objectives should be clearly stated, and the alternative means for achieving those objectives should be studied. It is especially important to conduct economic feasibility studies which analyze all costs, potential membership commitments, the extent of competition or alternative ways of accomplishing the stated objectives, opposition to be expected from various interest groups, available markets, suitable equipment needs, and the availability of leadership. Proper planning will cause enthusiasm to be tempered with the realities of the problems facing the coops. With much enthusiasm and limited planning, there is a danger that coops will be destroyed by unexpected adversities.

Few of the new cooperative enterprises have been preceded by careful planning and economic analysis. To some extent, this was because the coops often were formed in desperation to help people in difficult circumstances. The cooperative idea suggested itself as an alternative to the urban ghetto, and because of the experience with these organizations in other countries and among more affluent farmers in this country; it was not the product of careful analysis.

The Federation is attempting to correct these problems and has helped several of the new coops solve their planning and research needs by retaining consultants (economists, accountants, lawyers, management specialists, horticulturists, etc.) to work with these organizations. The Federation also has established its own research and resource development department which could undertake regular evaluations of the coops and investigate the feasibility of new cooperative ventures.

Role of Management

Above all, successful cooperatives, like other businesses, must have effective management. First of all, this requires competent and dedicated administrators. Moreover, because it must rely heavily on membership patronage, a healthy coop must adopt a structure which permits active membership participation and control, usually through boards of directors. In addition, the special economic, political, psychological, and social benefits to be derived from coops require effective interaction between members, boards of directors, and managers.

The poor people's coops formed in the rural South during the 1960s fall far short of these requirements. The founders of the coops were good organizers but poor administrators, and the recruitment of managers from the membership has been complicated by the members' low educational levels and lack of business experience. In addition, blacks with managerial training and experience are in very short supply in the rural South because they usually find better employment opportunities elsewhere.

However, effective management of the poor people's coops requires more than technical competence and training. Managers must be committed to the goals of the low-income coop movement and sensitive to the problems and needs of the rural poor. Indeed, the experience thus far seems to indicate that managers who are technically incompetent but dedicated may be more effective administrators than those who are highly skilled but undedicated. For example, two of the most highly educated and experienced managers almost destroyed two low-income coops because they did not devote sufficient time to their jobs and embezzled funds from the coops.

These experiences have caused SCDP and FSC leaders to conclude that it probably would be better to upgrade the managerial skills of members or others who are committed to fighting rural poverty, through training and education, than to import "outsiders." The SCDP and the Federation, therefore, have held a number of workshops for coop administrators, assigned field staff to work with individual members, hired consultants to provide on-the-job training, and have arranged for coop managers to participate in management classes and training sessions sponsored by such established groups as Midland Cooperatives and the Cooperative League of the U.S.A. The FSC also has arranged for its members to obtain training and technical assistance from Alcorn A&M College in Mississippi, Fort Valley University and Abraham Baldwin College in Georgia, Southern University in Louisiana, and Tuskegee Institute in Alabama. In the summer of 1970 the Federation had been promised help from Clemson University, the University of Georgia, and the University of Florida. In addition, the FSC has sent managers and members of its field staff to Israel, where they are receiving training from that country's coop leaders. This exchange program was sponsored by the HISTRADRUT, the Israeli National Federation of Labor Organization.

In providing training for the coops' boards of directors, the SCDP and the Federation have made extensive use of "sensivity" and T-group methods provided on a contractual basis by the Scholarship Education and Defense Fund for Racial Equality (SEDFRE). The purpose of these sessions was either to help board members overcome their feelings of inferiority or to settle internal conflicts and factional struggles.

Another important requirement for management success is sound accounting. Accurate records which reveal the financial health and problems of the coop are essential to the development of effective management policy and control by boards and members. In a low-income coop this also means that regular financial reports must be presented in such a manner that poorly educated members can understand them.

Virtually all of the low-income coops in the South have had record-keeping difficulties. Many members, even those who are on the boards of directors, do not understand their coop's financial statements or are afraid to question managers about financial matters. Few of the coops have regular bookkeepers, and some kept no records at all.

The FSC has helped most of its member coops overcome some of their accounting difficulties mainly through the use of consultants. The Federation also has a full-time credit union specialist on its staff who makes regular visits to the credit unions to help them with accounting and bookkeeping problems. In the summer of 1970 a proposal was pending with the U.S. Department of Labor for a one million dollar grant to establish a management training program for coop administrators.

MARKETING

All of the low-income agricultural cooperatives have been plagued by marketing problems. One of the major causes of these difficulties has been the lack of market intelligence. Very few of the coop leaders, managers, and other personnel know much about such dynamics of agricultural markets as how to make credit checks on brokers in distant locations and other "tricks of the trade." It has been very difficult for the leaders of the low-income coops to develop the formal and informal contacts which are so essential in this activity. As a result, some coops have been swindled by unscrupulous produce brokers to whom they had shipped produce on consignment. Although legal action was taken, none of this money was recovered because the brokers went out of business. All businesses suffer from these problems, but their impact on marginal enterprises is much greater. In other cases, coops have suffered because they waited until the last minute to attempt to locate markets instead of developing advanced market plans. Some coops have purchased produce which had to be burned because it could not be marketed.

Marketing problems also stem from the inability of some of the agricultural coops to obtain sufficient volume to compete with private processors and attract large buyers. Membership participation in the form of active use of the coops' services has not been as great as it must be if the coops are to survive and become economically viable. Membership participation, especially in Alabama and Louisiana, has been limited by harassment from local political and economic leaders who have threatened or bribed potential coop members. Moreover, according to some observers, fatalism and conservatism have kept some rural blacks from actively supporting self-help organizations. Some poor farmers, especially those who have worked on white plantations for most of their lives, have serious doubts about the ability of blacks to succeed in business activities. These skeptics view the struggling coops as simply another in the long line of panaceas which have come and gone without changing their material well-being. It will take sustained and demonstrated success to overcome these attitudes. But perhaps the main reason many low-income farmers have not patronized the coops is that they have not seen any economic advantage in doing so. As mentioned earlier, some of the coops are so financially weak that they have been unable to pay farmers for produce upon delivery or render the kinds of services (advance payments, etc.) available from private traders. People with incomes which average only about $1,000 a year—a third of the poverty standard—cannot be expected to make economic sacrifices in order to keep the coops alive.

The agricultural coops also have had marketing difficulties because of quality control problems due to improper grading procedures and inadequate or insufficient processing equipment and storage facilities. This is partly because of the undercapitalization and management problems discussed previously. SWAFCA, for example, did not complete the construction of its field collection stations until its inefficient manager was replaced, and Grand Marie's volume suffered because of crop shrinkage and deterioration caused by temperature control problems in its dilapidated storage sheds. The solution to these problems is obvious. The coops need more and better machinery and facilities, and this requires better financing.

Inferior quality produce also has resulted from improper farming practices. Many of the members of the new coops are learning to produce crops they have never grown before, and they have not yet mastered the most efficient cultivation methods. Failure to use good seed or fertilizer, to keep crops dry and clean until delivered, or to plant and harvest on time are good examples of this. The coops have found it extremely difficult to refuse substandard produce for fear that this would alienate members.

The SCDP and the Federation have done a number of things to help the agricultural cooperatives with their marketing problems. Both organizations have retained consultants to help individual coops, and the Federation employed a produce marketing specialist on its central staff to help several of the coops develop marketing plans, select brokers, develop sales contacts, and negotiate contracts with food processors. The Federation also has helped small farmers improve their farming techniques through training programs and has helped its member coops obtain crop insurance and transportation services. For example, some of the coops are shipping their produce in government surplus trucks obtained through the Federation.

In short, the Federation is attempting to fill the gap left by the federal government's failure to implement programs to help poor farmers, but its resources, staff, and experiences are too limited to do the job that needs to be done for the entire South. Indeed, it is difficult to see how the job will be done adequately without a fundamental revision in the federal agricultural and welfare policies, and this is not likely to be done until poor farmers and agricultural workers and their allies acquire enough political power to threaten the agricultural establishment.

The Federation's leaders are aware of these difficulties and what is required to overcome them and is documenting discrimination in federal programs which will be published and presented to Congress. FSC also provides legal counsel to coops and individuals who file complaints against government agencies.

CREDIT SUPPLY

Even if coops are based on felt needs, adopt the proper organizational forms, and attract competent managers and technical assistance, they, like other business enterprises, still need sources of credit to cover emergencies and take advantage of income-earning opportunities. Credit sources are particularly important to permit small farmers to buy land. Ideally, coops should raise at least half of their funds from their members in order to avoid a heavy debt structure and give members a stake in the enterprise. Actually, however, the members of the new poor people's coops have provided a small proportion of their capital needs. The main reason for this limited membership investment is the very low incomes and assets of the people involved.[1] Nevertheless, it probably would be much better for the cooperatives if their members were required to make sacrificial investments in them. Also, we favor a supervised credit approach, either for loans by the coops to their members or by government or other lending institutions to coops. Excessive reliance on grants could be dangerous, because grants do not necessitate the kind of economic discipline required to repay loans. Grants might also produce problems because the coops could suffer greatly from their inability to sustain the services made possible by the grants. A balance clearly needs to be struck between loans and grants to the poor people's coops. It probably also makes considerable difference what the loans and grants are used for. It would seem to be good practice to allocate loans for the purchase of tangibles (land, equipment) and grants for intangibles (professional services, educational activities).

Because they have so many managerial and financial problems, the low-income coops have great difficulty securing credit from traditional sources. Private institutions naturally try to maximize their profits and minimize their risks and can therefore find better investments than those provided by the struggling cooperatives and their members. Most commercial banks refuse to make loans to the coops, partly because they are risky but also because they oppose the idea of organizing coops among poor black farmers.

---

[1] For example, a tabulation of average assets, debts, and net worth for rural families from the Survey of Economic Opportunity made by the Office of Economic Opportunity in 1966 showed:

	Assets	Debts	Net Worth
White	$25,598	$4,724	$20,874
Negro	$ 4,639	$1,277	$ 3,362

Even those federal credit programs established for people who could not get credit from other sources often have not been willing to help low-income coops. The Banks for Cooperatives, initiated by the federal government in 1933 because established cooperatives were having trouble obtaining credit from traditional sources, have benefited wealthier coops by supplying technical services as well as credit. But the Banks for Cooperatives will provide only 50 percent of the funds for any loan application, and even this must be secured by collateral. The other 50 percent must be secured from other sources. The Banks for Cooperatives, like other federal agencies, thus are more useful to affluent farmers than to coops made up of poorer farmers.

The USDA program which has done the most for poor people's coops is the Opportunity Loan Program created in 1964 and administered by the FHA. These loans have played a major role in supporting the new poor people's coops, and some FHA representatives have been very helpful to poor farmers. We have noted, however, that FHA makes loans to the most affluent of the rural poor, has limited resources, is vulnerable to political pressures, and in many areas is administered by people who apparently are not always sympathetic to the growth of the poor people's coops. Moreover, neither the OEO or the FHA have relied on the supervised credit approach discussed in chapter 2, which we believe to be essential when dealing with the new coops.

As a result of the inadequacies of existing financial institutions, the FSC is attempting to launch a Southern Cooperative Development Fund to be financed from a combination of government, foundation, and private sources. The SCDF will make loans to cooperatives while the FSC renders technical assistance to help the coops use the loans more effectively. The new corporation is based on the belief that the proper mix between subsidized technical assistance and loans will vary with time and circumstances. The ratio of subsidies to loans will decline as the coop develops. It is expected that some coops can be developed to the point where they need no subsidies at all and can obtain loans from regular financial institutions, while others will need help for some time.

We therefore favor the creation of a federal rural development bank which would utilize the "supervised credit" approach discussed in chapter 2. Because such an organization probably would have limited resources, it should help its cooperative borrowers acquire as much leverage as possible through promoting revolving funds, loan guarantees, and pooling arrangements. The RDB should be in a position to minimize risks from rural activities, encourage business-like rural enterprises, and provide broad technical assistance. The RDB might be financed in much the same way as the original farm credit system, which permitted member organizations to retire federal stock. The bank could make loans to a wide variety of agencies and individuals engaged in job creation in rural areas.

FUTURE PROSPECTS

What are the prospects for the coops? This obviously is a difficult question to answer. If enough technical assistance can be rendered to make a few cooperatives successful in different areas, these organizations could become the center of additional activities or could at least stimulate the kinds of programs needed to permit people to make adequate livings and gain a measure of freedom in the rural South. If most of the present undertakings can be strengthened sufficiently to permit them to succeed, their efforts could have a multiplier effect because they could stimulate action by public and private agencies to help the rural poor as well as cause new coops to be formed.

But a number of objections have been raised to the coops. The first is that it is not at all clear that they are economically desirable or feasible. The desirability is questioned by those who argue that it will not be possible to provide adequate economic opportunities for poor people in the rural South. As noted earlier, in this view, small farmers are not likely to be able to compete with larger mechanized farms. Blacks are at a particular disadvantage, according to these critics, because they own very little land, are uneducated, lack managerial experience, and have inadequate finan-

95

cial resources. Moreover, in this view, the solution to rural poverty is not to keep people on the farm but to increase their productivity and get them into good nonagricultural jobs.

The answer to all of this is that we have no assurance of the economic feasibility of poor people's cooperatives and are aware of the difficulties involved in making them self-supporting. Moreover, few people would argue that coops alone are permanent solutions to the problems of the rural poor. Many other specific programs are necessary to really improve their conditions; it is our contention that coops are simply one approach which can help poor farmers increase their productivity and incomes. Southern agriculture is going to provide good incomes to a lot of people, some of whom can and should be black. In the absence of coops or programs to provide similar services, few small farmers, black or white, are likely to survive. Even if coops are not successful in becoming completely self-sufficient, they can provide means for small farmers to survive with subsidies—which currently are being given to larger farmers and many businesses. Indeed, it is not at all clear how much the growth of large farms in the South is due to federal subsidies and how much to the economies of scale. However, the evidence suggests that large farmers have advantages under the American system in certain crops which can be mechanized but that small farms also have advantages, as noted in chapter 1. Clearly, the efficiency of farm cooperatives is more important than size. The open question is whether coops can induce sufficient efficiency to make small farms viable. Moreover, small farmers can use agriculture as a means to supplement welfare or earnings in rural nonfarm industries. In essence, therefore, some of these coops can be economic organizations with welfare components whose viability is derived from rendering a variety of economic and noneconomic services to their members.

Nor are the coops designed to keep people down on the farm. They are based on the belief that many people, especially those who are older and less well educated, are going to work in marginal enterprises wherever they go and that even some who could make higher incomes in cities will prefer to remain on the farm, especially if there are leadership positions available to them. The coops therefore are designed to increase the options available to the rural poor either in farming or small enterprises.

Marginal economic enterprises like cooperatives also are criticized because they operate on a scale which is likely to be insignificant to those accustomed to dealing with more profitable organizations. A net increase in incomes of from $300 to $500 a year for each family, which is estimated to be the net gain from the FHA's economic opportunity loan program, might cause these enterprises to be considered failures by those accustomed to urban standards. However, for people who average between $800 and $1,000 a year, an increase of $300 can be very significant. In many rural areas, people who earn $3,000 a year are relatively well off. With coops and the Family Assistance Plan, many of them could attain this level. It should be emphasized, moreover, that these cooperatives cannot be judged in economic terms alone and that, as development organizations, they could provide for continuous advancements in incomes.

It might also be argued that the coops are not likely to be politically feasible in view of the opposition to them from powerful southern congressional interests. The leaders of the rural poor are well aware of the political obstacles they face but hope they can gain enough allies in other parts of the country and among southerners outside the agricultural establishment to get sufficient assistance for their programs from federal, state, and local governments. Moreover, they hope the growth of voter registration and the economic security provided by federally administered welfare programs will give them sufficient independence to influence public institutions. As noted in chapters 3 and 4, many of the coops already have had political influence in their communities.

In order to become economically viable in the long run, coops must also be productive and efficient enough to compete with private firms. This means that their economic operations must be based on the latest technology or must be in activities which are labor intensive and not subject to mechanization. But, in the long run, the areas protected from mechanization and agribusiness apparently are going to be very limited indeed.[2] In many areas, therefore, coops must be able to acquire necessary financial resources to obtain equipment that will make it possible for their members to become more productive, to diversify, and therefore to compete with agribusinesses. If small farmers adapt to modern technology, it will have to be through some organizational form like the coop. If they fail to acquire the technology, they will only be able to compete if they continue to be subsidized or are willing to accept lower incomes to offset their inefficiency. If the coops acquire the equipment and develop, they can have a significant impact on the incomes of small farmers. Otherwise, they will be temporary welfare programs to make it possible for older poor farmers to live out their lives on the land. Only developmental coops based on efficient management and advanced technology will be able to attract younger people into farming and staff positions. The coops hope to become developmental, but it is too early to say with much confidence that they will.

[2] See B. F. Cargill and G. E. Rossmiller (eds.), *Fruit and Vegetable Harvest Mechanization*, Rural Manpower Center (East Lansing: Michigan State University Press, 1969).